Toddler Tips:

The Complete Parenting Guide With Proven Strategies To Understand And Managing Toddler's Behavior, Dealing With Tantrums, And Reach An Effective Communication With Kids

Author

Lisa Marshall

3

is provided beforehand. Any additional rights reserved.

Furthermore, the information that can be found within the pages described forthwith shall be considered both accurate and truthful when it comes to the recounting of facts. As such, any use, correct or incorrect, of the provided information will render the Publisher free of responsibility as to the actions taken outside of their direct purview. Regardless, there are zero scenarios where the original author or the Publisher can be deemed liable in any fashion for any damages or hardships that may result from any of the information discussed herein.

Additionally, the information in the following pages is intended only for informational purposes and should thus be thought of as universal. As befitting its nature, it is presented without assurance regarding its prolonged validity or interim quality. Trademarks that are mentioned are done without written consent and can in no way be considered an endorsement from the trademark holder.

Thank you for purchasing this book!

Click on this link to download this FREE tool

http://bit.ly/childrenbehaviortips

Note: If you have purchased the paperback format then you need to write this link on your browser search bar. This tool is a useful resource to understand childrens behavior. It is also a quick guide to connect and respond effectively to your child. All in all, it is a fundamental tool that will help you become an expert on parenting!!

Table of Contents

Preface

If you are reading this, I assume you probably
have been dealing with a lot of stress or anxieties
that parents often go through, like dealing with
the "Terrible Twos", poor child's behavior,
tantrums, and all sources of common parenting
problems. We love our kids so much, even though
they sometimes drive us crazy. Their behaviors
and actions make us worry that we aren't doing
enough to raise them properly. I've heard a lot of
mums and dads feeling frustrated that they are
failing as parents, and I know, you want peace and
quietness back in your home. You're not alone, in
fact, you are in very good company. The good
news is that you can get the changes you want. My
experience proves you can actually turn things
around to enjoy your kids and your time as a
parent, much more than you are right now. I'd
like to help you make those changes by showing
you some of the most important tools you can
learn to make this a success.

Here is the good news; most of the problems
you're facing with your child's behavior are not
your fault. Think about it, kids come without an
instruction manual and, nobody trains us on how
to actually deal with toddlers and preschoolers.
They don't teach this stuff in school and when

you're expecting your first child, you may have to take on those parenting classes to have an insight on what to expect; the session that teaches you how to hold baby, how to feed a baby and everything involved in taking care of a baby! Sure it's important stuff, but it's actually pretty easy compared to the "terrible twos". This is a big source for stressed parents, as you can learn and apply better ways to deal with your kids. There is only one real reason you don't have a peaceful home you want with your well-behaved children.

Number 1: Behavior is driven by emotion, not logic. This is the basis of the entire process. The behavior of any person of any age is determined by their emotional state. People act from their emotion and they later justify the action with logic. But little kids don't have the ability to use logic, so they act purely from emotion. Let's say that your child won't get to dress in the morning, or eat his dinner, or won't share a toy with a playmate. Your child mentally connects their behavior to some kind of emotional pain, and so no matter how many times you ask, they won't collaborate. Changing your child's emotional state is the key to getting the behavior you would want to see in them. So how do you change your child's emotional state? I discovered some very specific language patterns to make it easier for your child to feel good about the kind of behavior you would want them to display. Once they feel good about it, the behavioral changes follow instantly. I have seen so many parents trying to use logic on their children; "If you eat that cookie, you won't be hungry for dinner," or "If you don't wear this coat, you will be cold outside!" This logic simply doesn't work. You can validate this by thinking about your own experiences with your child.

Number 2: We tend to overuse the word "NO" when we talk to our kids. You remember the story of the boy who cried "wolf" many times, right? When a parent cries out "no" to every little thing, kids stop listening. People including kids are programmed to notice differences. If you driving down the road, you tend not to notice the normal behaviors of other cars or people walking on the sidewalk. But if a car suddenly comes to a stop or the child suddenly runs to the street, you do take notice because something is different. If you say "no" so often, it will be fade in the background, becoming ordinary as cars on the road or people on the sidewalk. The better alternative is to change your child's behavior without using "no" all the time. I will show you how exactly you can do this using language techniques that seem almost magical and almost too easy!

Number 3: If you want to have any chance at all influencing your child's behavior, first, you must have rapport! "Rapport" simply means having an emotional connection with another person. This is why when strangers are talking about the weather or gasoline prices, they are consciously making general comments they know the other person will agree with. The agreement creates rapport. It's a natural process that all we do in our relationships, but we also forget that we need to build rapport with our kids too. I'll show you lots of ways to create this crucial emotional bridge before you can change a child's behavior.

Number 4: Language is a powerful tool and there are a bunch of tactics you need to learn to create occurrences you want. Here a specific tip: Use positive language instead of negative language. Ask your child to sit down instead of not jumping on the couch. Tell him/her "Behold your cup into hands" instead of "Don't spill your milk." This is the opposite that most of us speak. It is scientifically proven that speaking in negative terms is insanely what you don't want. Who actually causes your child to do exactly what you trying to avoid? You want some subtle prove on what works for you right now? Okay, do not think of the colors of your child's hair right now. Don't think about it and certainly don't form a mental image of it right now. Seen? As soon as you are told not to do something, you at least think about it, so you can understand what it is that you aren't supposed to do. The difference is that young kids, unlike adults, don't have what I call critical faculty, which helps to process negative language. I've got some more information to share. Can you imagine what will happen if you install a powerful set of communication strategies within your mind? It's not as hard as you might think, and the effects are fast and powerful. How much peaceful will be your life once you know how to fix or even prevent most of these behavioral problems you've been dealing with. Would you love to start enjoying more and smile with your kids? One real thing you can understand is knowing that you're doing the best job you can to make their lives better. I want you to either experience the joy of loving and nurturing an emotionally healthy family life. It's entirely achievable because I've helped thousands of other parents learn how to deal with their kids more effectively. There are still far too many parents who share the same frustrations and need these solutions.

I think it is best to share my story with you so you can understand why I feel so passionate to share these parenting strategies with you. My name is Lisa Marshall and I'm graduated as an expert in communication psychology. One day, the university invited a guest speaker and that went on to change my life forever. The speaker showed us how to use our brain to make powerful shifts in our emotional states, he also discussed the basics of influence, persuasion and relationship building. This stuff really excited me. I would fall in love with this kind of argument, and I finished from school to become an expert in this field. After some years I met my husband and in two years, we had our first child. Since then, in that first moment, holding this tiny baby of mine, it always hit me that I had much more responsibility than ever before. By the time he was entering the terrible twos, I was pregnant again with my second daughter. Here, my training started to come in and things were bearing me so far. The challenges and problems we faced will end in a very typical way. This is where I found the idea that my knowledge in the relationships and influencing people could probably work on small children too. The tools just needed to be reworked, with the help of exhaustive research in the field of children, and for five years, I started connections and cooperations with many experts in this field. I took the time to take my communication skills and I adapted to them so well. I would reuse them for children, and what I developed is a unique effective toolbox for parents. I have always been a natural teacher, so after experimenting on my own kids, I started working with other parents. The results were truly spectacular!

Parents no longer felt like being out of control. Kids started to behave better as the results were fast, and best of all, the strategies I teach maintains a child's dignity and actually help the child to understand how to make better choices. I turned all of this in the book you are going to read called *"Toddler Discipline Tips."* The techniques you'll learn will work on any age group and not just toddlers. This book is unique because it is the only program that breaks up the science of communication and applies to the kids with the parent-approved emphasis on creating a positive influence on children.

"Children must be taught how to think, not what to think"

Margaret Mead-

Introduction

Congratulations on downloading *Toddler Discipline Tips,* and thank you for doing so.

There are plenty of books on this subject on the market, thanks again for choosing this one! Every effort was made to ensure it is full of as much useful information as possible. Please enjoy!

It's important that we introduce an understanding of positive discipline before approaching behavior as a whole. This book will teach you what positive discipline is, from when to apply it to how to do it properly.
Positive discipline is a new method that is used to look after babies and children in a different way by using a different point of view. While in the traditional discipline we speak of punishing wrong behavior, in the positive discipline, we keep in mind the type of adult we want to create and what would be the reaction of society to that mistake.

Thus, positive discipline is a form of non-punitive discipline that favors self-esteem, the independence of the child, and the bond between parents and children.

How To Act When The Baby Or Child Does Something Wrong

You must be thinking, if this discipline is not punitive, how will I act when my child does something wrong? Well, it would be just like when adults do something wrong. If you make mistakes in your work, you have to bear the consequences of your mistake, sometimes financial, sometimes moral, and whenever possible, you have to correct the mistake. So the child learns to correct something that he or she has done wrong.

So if your child hits another child, for example, applying positive discipline will teach the child to understand the problems that this has caused to the other child. The child has to learn to think of other people, to have empathy. Based on that empathy, you need to teach the child to see their mistakes and correct them whenever possible. It has no punishment, and it has no scolding, but everything depends on the patience of the parents.

Of course, this question of understanding the consequences of their mistakes applies to older children as well. In the case of babies, it is different. At that age, there is not much language. However, parents can start saying short sentences, like 'no, that hurts.' If the baby wants something that he or she cannot have, you need to take the object away from the line of sight so that it stops being the focus. If the baby cries because of this, parents should comfort the child but under no circumstances should they deliver the object to the child and let them have what was forbidden.

When the baby is one year and a few months old, they already understand what the adults say. So parents can better explain why something cannot be done. Thus, positive discipline from this age is made up of many conversations and explanations about why certain things cannot be done.

When the child does something that the parents did not like, they should never say things like: you are a pest. Parents should make it clear that they did not like the child's attitude by saying something like: It is not cool to beat your friend because it hurts him. This method has very firm limits and at the same time, offers freedom to the child. It is similar to society, where there are general laws, but people are free.

How To Act When The Baby Or Child Does Something Right

In traditional discipline, when the child does something right, the parents usually show appreciation. However, when he or she does something wrong, the parents express displeasure. In positive discipline, it is different. It's important that parents try to show that they have noticed good behavior and praise it. It is also important to praise the effort of the child.

When To Begin With Positive Discipline

During the baby's early months, there is little point in applying positive discipline. From around 8 or 9 months, the baby has a developmental leap and learns to communicate by crying. It's a complicated phase because until this point there was no action of disciplining the child and now they insist on what they want. So from this point on, we can apply positive discipline.

Tips For Applying Positive Discipline

One of the most important tips for applying positive discipline is to never lie to the child. For example: if your child wants a cookie, but you do not want to give him or her that cookie, do not say that there is no cookie in order to avoid explanations. You also have to avoid bribery and blackmail because if you do that, the child always screams and cries. If the rule exists, it has to be valid.

Another great tip is to think well before saying no. After all, in this method, it is not acceptable that parents change their mind after the child's insistence. Parents have to take the blame for their own behavior. You must lead by example.

Benefits Of Positive Discipline

Positive discipline helps children to become creative adults. In this method, we do not punish the error, but rather correct it. As opposed to punishment, that creates in children the fear of making mistakes.

The child's self-esteem is stimulated with positive discipline. In this method, we encourage learning to reward achievements. For example, if your child wants a bike and you give it to him or her the same day, the child has nothing to wait for. So it's interesting that parents set a date for him or her to get the bike, for example, her birthday.

Positive discipline has a number of positive effects on the confidence of the child. This book will help you understand how to discipline your child without using fear as a weapon.

Chapter 1: Understanding Toddler Behavior

Toddlers are difficult to understand for even the most patient and nurturing adult. Keeping a positive outlook and going easy on yourself on the difficult days is imperative. What if your child bites his little friend, or throws food on the floor and starts yelling? How do we prepare ourselves to deal with this moment? The idea, of course, is to always opt for the path of a good education. To do this, we talked to some experts, who suggested ways to deal with children for bad behaviors.

Deciphering child behavior is not an easy task for parents. The quest for answers often runs counter to the way they raise their children, the amount of "no" they can say to them, within the limits they can impose. Often, adults sense how they should act, but the fear of frustrating children ultimately results in resignation. Indeed, children have standard attitudes in every stage of life, but that does not mean that adults have to follow orders and accept all attacks as something natural in the development process. To help parents act during difficult times, we sought out child education and behavioral experts who suggested ways to understand toddler behavior.

Up To 2 Years Old

1. My child has the habit of biting people. How do we teach him that this is wrong? It's expected by professionals who deal with children that they will bite until they are 3 or 4 years old, but adults cannot allow them to bite, because it hurts and it's wrong. By the time your child bites a classmate or anyone else, the professional counsels the good old eye-to-eye conversation. Stay at the same height as the child and speak firmly that this cannot and should not happen because it hurts. Parents have to make it clear that they do not approve of this behavior because even though they do not have clear notions of right and wrong, they cannot do everything they want. This does not mean that behavior does not repeat itself, but every time it occurs, it is necessary to make your position clear.

2. What do I do to stop my child from crying? Children below 2 years of age have no resourceful means of communicating, so constant crying indicates discomfort, physical or emotional, that needs to be investigated by the doctor. As the baby does not know how to speak, they use crying to demonstrate that they're suffering. From the age of 2, however, the child already realizes how he or she can manipulate their parents and uses crying to try to get what they want. I believe that one of the ways to help your child to learn to cope with frustration is by disregarding their desires when they come along with the temper tantrums.

3. How should I act in the face of a raging attack by my child in public places or if he kicks when he is not served?

The suggestion here is to try to prevent the child from seeing your frustration. If necessary, you should hug the child from behind to contain him or her. This way, you do not show your annoyance. Tell them that their behavior is wrong, that you do not approve of the way they act. If it does not work and he or she is not in danger, I suggest that the parents move away and allow the child to get their energy out. Most people have spent time with children and will have some understanding of what you are going through. Do not feel embarrassed or like a failure as a parent. We've all been there. Once your child realizes that their behavior will not get them the desired result, he or she will stop.

4. My son loves to slap his face and pull people's hair. What should I tell him at those times?

Though there are times when this can be amusing, it's best to never give that kind of attention to this type of thing. The behavior should not be tolerated. Hold the baby's hand(do not laugh or make a face that shows you become sad when this happens). It is by observing the reaction of others that children learn to interpret feelings and develop empathy for others. Always speak of your feelings. Never use negative terms about your child like bad or ugly. And do not fall into the trap of spanking. If you do, you will be reinforcing the learning of physical aggression, which is a bad example.

5. When displeased, my son begins to scream. How can I show that this is wrong?
Is this child learning this behavior from you? If you cannot control yourself, the child may just be repeating what he sees. Think about it. Accepting frustrations is a major difficulty nowadays for parents and children. How often do you get frustrated that you do not earn more or that you are not recognized at work as you should?

With an older child, you can pretend you do not know and leave her screaming on her own. If you leave, you will see that she will not repeat the same thing again. In the case of small ones, the solution is to try to calm them down. Hug the child from behind, be quiet, and make sounds like 'Ssshhhh' in her ear.

6. My 1-year-old son, when irritated, bangs his head on the floor or wall. How should I act?
If the child is at risk of injury, you must hold the child and stop the action by hugging from behind. It is worth trying the technique of making the 'Ssshhhh' sound in the ear and asking him to calm down. If none of this works and he continues to make this action, you must seek the help of a doctor. Self-harm is not acceptable behavior and can indicate serious mental disorders and needs an assessment from a psychiatrist.

7. My 1-year-old and 2-month-old baby test my patience every day. Should I show him what he

can or cannot do? Does he already understand the concept of right and wrong?

He may not distinguish between right and wrong, but at this age, he begins to perceive inconsistencies. How often do children at this stage test their parents? When they do something, they look at them and hear the no; they do it again until the father or mother asks to stop the act. And they repeat this many times, demonstrating that they have a certain notion of what is important.

Over 2 Years Old

1. My daughter is throwing tantrums in public places, such as shopping. How shall I rebuke her? Children with this kind of recurring behavior have no limits and may feel devoid of affection and attention. This is not to say that parents do not love them, just that they may not know how to demonstrate it. Another reason is that many parents fail to understand the role of frustration and fear. They may feel they're not deserving of love unless they do everything for their children. In the process, they end up creating people who are not satisfied with anything. The first step to answering this question then is to take a step back and examine how the tantrums come about, how you deal with them, and how you and your child feel throughout the process. By having empathy for your child and formulating a concrete plan to

deal with tantrums, your child will know what to expect, and you will know what to do.

2. When it comes to playing, my son prefers dolls and girl clothes to cars and men's clothing. Is there a problem with that?
Playing is a fantasy and is the way to unload in the imaginary world what they cannot do in real life. Although boys may end up playing with a doll, this is nothing more than the exercise of care. You should celebrate your child's sense of caring, just as you would a little girl.

3. My son likes to play, pretend that he kills people. For a long time, I avoided buying toy weapons, but he turns any object into a revolver. Should I stick to the ban?
People often confuse the fantasy world and reality. Although your problem is common, if you feel it is becoming too real, then go with your gut. Since your child is interested in the weapons, playing new games that involve them is a great way to become more comfortable. Guns can be used for chasing bad guys, shooting water to win a prize, popping bubbles, or shooting aliens with lasers. Think like a child, and the possibilities are endless!

4. My son is very shy. He is ashamed to play with other children. How can I encourage him to interact with others?
Being introspective, quieter, having few friends, is not a problem, but a temperament, and is a part of the personality. Extraversion can also be a

source of distress. Parents should only worry if the child cannot relate, participate in collective games, or dislikes being with other people. In that case, you must seek the help of a professional. If you feel your child could use a little push, you can try and get other children involved with his interests. For example, bring several match cars to the park and see if other children would like to race them down the slide with him, or bring chalk and bubbles.

5. Sometimes I blackmail to convince my son to take a shower or change clothes. Am I acting correctly?
Bathing, brushing teeth, sitting at the table to eat, and taking vaccines are mandatory. But by the age of two, for example, the child begins to claim possession over his own body. One suggestion for when he or she does not want to bathe is to play the game of self-help, giving tools and negotiating: you buy a nice sponge, a special soap and let them wash with your supervision.

6. When I go out with my son, he always asks me to buy something (a toy, for example). If I do not buy it, he throws a tantrum. How should I act?
At 2 years of age, the child believes that everything is his. Then the parents take him to a lovely place, like a toy store. Put yourself in the place of the little one and imagine yourself in a place with everything that you like without being able to take anything. To avoid a scene, it is recommended talking to the little one before

leaving the house and determining if there will be new acquisitions.

7. When I go out to dinner, my son does not sit quietly at the table. He runs around the restaurant and bothers everyone. Should I rebuke him?
You should most definitely not allow this to continue. Though all children have different energy levels, it is disrespectful and rude to allow your kids to run around. The toddler years are important for growing social skills, and you set the standard. Interact with your child at the table. Bring playdough and crayons, play 'I Spy,' and talk about things that interest them. As they grow, they will learn to entertain themselves healthily because you put the time into building their self-esteem.

The Only Child And The Arrival Of The Younger Sibling

You love your children the same way, but do your little ones think the same thing? The impact of the arrival of a younger sibling in the family is intense for the parents but especially for the children. Girls tend to identify with mothers, while boys tend to be more reserved. They will touch the mother's abdomen and agree to hear the baby's heart. They get excited about becoming the older brother or sister, but then comes the sudden split of your attention. Preparing your child for the arrival of your new baby is certainly worthwhile.

Before the baby is born, you can set up your nursery and allow the firstborn to get to know the new routine. Get a doll and show your child what it will be like to change, feed, and rock the baby. Practice being quiet and gentle. Though your child will not be able to care for the new baby, he/she can continue caring for the doll, as well as helping you by getting things that you need.

Though this newfound sense of responsibility is useful in building self-esteem, your older child is still just that – a child. Setting up a spot for you and the older child is a wonderful practice since there will be times that he/she needs your attention. It could be as simple as a chair that you two sit on to talk, a blanket for only you two, or a reading corner. Allowing your child to feel in control of their relationship with you can help deter from regressive behaviors developing, due to the new baby. Remember to positive reinforcement by complimenting your child on how well he/she is doing as an older sibling. Tell them how much you enjoy having a big boy or girl around!

Children Having Trouble Sleeping

Children need at least eight hours of sleep. Children are different in their sleeping habits, but all toddlers enjoy having a routine. Bath time is one of the best ways to get your child ready for bed. If your schedule doesn't allow for that, then you can look into reading a set number of books or watching a quiet cartoon. Some children benefit from a favorite stuffed animal or blanket. These things are comforting and can make a child feel safe. If the problem is staying asleep, you may want to look into a sound machine. There are so many light/sound machines on the market that you're sure to find one that suits your taste.

As your child grows, they are bound to have different excuses for not wanting to go to bed on time. Nightmares are a common occurrence in little ones and extremely frightening to deal with in the beginning. Take the time to explain that they are not real and teach them how to handle it on their own. Talking about something that made them happy that day, every night can double as their special tool to calm them if a nightmare occurs.

Above all else, if you want your household to enjoy restful sleep, establish ground rules, and stick to them.

The Sexuality Of Children

It is in the age range of five years that the child reaches a stage of development in which it differs as the figure of the man as the father, and the figure of the female the woman similar to the mother and understands the ties of relations of the outside world. However, even when the child already has a clear idea of female and male genders, it still raises doubts about their sexual identity.

At first, children will move according to the world, at home or in society, in a spontaneous way. It is only when parents or others express their idea that they are doing something that is not right that the child will suddenly or gradually perceive a conflict between their inclinations and the way adults expect them to behave.

Allowing children to explore their interests freely permits them to become who they want to be, sexuality aside. Pressuring a child to like certain gender-specific toys or mannerisms may have the opposite effect, and can lead to frustration.

Divorce: How Children Handle The Separation Of Parents

A divorce causes suffering and, in many cases, long-term problems for the children, whether psychological or social. This is because, no matter how much the couple believes in conveying harmony to their children, they are more likely to perceive conflicts.

Ideally, a couple who are divorcing should be able to maintain some degree of friendship that can make their lives less traumatic. Good sense and simple human respect are helpful. However, in the vast majority of cases, these qualities are ignored by one partner or both, which can start an irrational battle. The best solution: "Seek a psychotherapist, therapist, or marriage counselor to find a middle ground and a place to communicate well".

5 Psychology Tips to Understand Child Behavior

A child that cries non-stop cannot sleep alone, does not get along with his classmates at school is a child who could have behavioral problems. These characteristics in children worry parents, however, those are typical child behaviors. Children have a way of communicating by crying, expressing their aggression and fears with behaviors that may seem like mischief.

Let's take a look at 5 tips recommended by psychologists to handle some of these behavior issues, without having to despair or be aggressive with children.

1. Constant Crying

Children crying is often seen as tantrums or stubbornness. But that depends on the age of your child. When a child is less than 2 years old, crying is a way to communicate something that is not going well.

At this stage, a child cries because some physical or emotional aspect is causing discomfort. So it's good to look for a doctor or specialist rather than ignoring or trying to correct him or her. The tantrum phase and manipulation by crying usually begin after two years of age.

After age two, you'll need to be patient and have an understanding of your child's feelings. Having good communication and compassion can go a long way in changing their behavior.

2. Difficulties In Sleeping

Does your child delay sleep, even if he/she had a tiring day? Does he usually watch TV to try to sleep? If the answer is "yes," then it may be that the use of this device interferes with the quality of the child's sleep. This is because the luminosity emitted by television hinders the release of the hormone melatonin that is important for sleep. If your child watches a scary movie that intrigues or frightens him, it can cause his mind to stay awake and be anxious. Replace TV and movies with a book. Read to your child and discover the importance of this habit.

3. Fear Of Darkness

You put your child in bed, give him a goodnight kiss, and turn out the light of the room. Ready! That's where the crying and the fear of sleeping in the dark begins. This behavior is very natural.

At this stage, the child's behavior is guided by a very fertile imagination, able to create the famous monsters that attack the child while the lights are off.

Leave a low-intensity dim light or nightlight on in the room or adopt other methods such as talking more with the child, so she will be calmer. As time goes by, your child will realize that those monsters do not exist.

4. Aggressiveness

Does your child tease or hit other children? Or siblings even? This childish behavior must be viewed with care. Aggressiveness is part of our psyche; for it not to have major consequences, it must be worked on early.

When your child hits someone, talk to him. Ask him why he did it. It is crucial that a child learn to reflect and express his anger using words.

5. Fear Of Strangers

You need to work, so you put your child in a daycare that you trust. But he cries a lot and does not want to stay there at all. This type of behavior is normal because the child still has a very close relationship and is dependent on the parents. Hence there is the fear of abandonment.

In this case, you can spend time with your child at the daycare center, introducing the teacher and colleagues until he feels more confident. Then explain to your child that you need to go to work and that you will leave him with someone you know.

You can also leave your child with uncles, aunts, and grandparents. He will feel more secure and improve the bonds of affection with his relatives.

Chapter 2: Encouraging Good Toddler Behavior

One of the most effective ways to encourage positive behavior in children is through praise. Children seek love and recognition for their efforts and progress. Praise increases children's self-confidence and motivation by making them feel happy. It is important to give them confidence in their abilities and to show them that they feel proud when they behave correctly, thereby encouraging good behavior. Here are some highly effective tips to help encourage positive behavior.

Encourage Effort

Use praise to encourage effort and to enhance the progress of your child. A child who can use the bathroom alone for the first time or perform a task that he was not able to do before deserves recognition. In this way, it is encouraging the child's development and autonomy.

Reinforce Attitudes

Enjoy instilling some values that you consider fundamental, important, and positive. By praising and reinforcing attitudes, you help to develop social skills that will make relationships easier in the future.

Praise the Effort, Regardless of the Result
The effort must be praised even if the goal is not fully achieved. If your child did not receive an excellent grade, but studied and worked for this to be possible, it is important to recognize him. Praise is key to staying motivated and therefore improving your bottom line.

Praise Good Behavior
It is important to praise good behavior; do not save compliments only for great achievements. Small behavior improvements should also be valued. If we only pay attention at times where behavior needs work, children will feel inclined to do wrong.

Approve or Disregard Attitudes and Not the Child
As much as you consider your child to be very handsome, intelligent, etc., avoid telling him this often. This type of label turns out to be as harmful as the opposite ("you're dumb," "you're bad," etc.). Try to mark your approval or disapproval regarding attitudes, not the child.

Value the Achievements of the Family
It is important to value the achievements and efforts of the family. If a brother has conquered something, it is important to praise him, as well, the achievements of the father or mother. It is important to recognize the effort of all the

elements and celebrate the achievements in the family.

Rewards

You can also choose to reward your child, such as a gift, a trip to the movies, or candy if you want to reinforce an attitude. But do not make it a routine, because this can lead to only good behavior when rewarded. Most behavior should be rewarded only by praise. Also, you may be tempted to use the allowance as a reward. We do not recommend it. Never use the allowance to "buy" your child.

Rewarding the child for good behavior teaches them to understand that there is a direct link between action and consequence.

Remember that as a parent you are a role model for your children. It is essential that you be a good role model by providing them with appropriate rules and standards to follow. Consistency is the key. Children learn by observing others, and they will learn these qualities. With a little persuasion and positive reinforcement, you can teach, encourage, and create positive behavior in children.

How To Stimulate Good Behavior In Children

Educating our children was not easy. So I went after tips on how to encourage good behavior in children without having to punish and scold every second.

Stimulating good behavior in children is one of the best ways to impose limits, without having to apply punishments constantly. The only problem is how to do that. In most cases, our little ones tested our limits and seem to do anything not to obey.

Here are ways to stimulate good behavior:

Be The Example

Being an example is the most effective way we have to teach our children anything - both good and bad. When it comes to encouraging good behavior in children, it is no different. Here are a few examples of what you can do for your child to learn.

Catch your child's attention when you split snacks with your husband or when you have to wait in the bank queue, pointing out that adults also have to share and wait too.

Realize The Good Behavior

If you are like any parent in the world when your child is behaving well, you leave him playing alone and take advantage of the time to do anything you may need to. But when your child is behaving badly, you direct all your attention to him to resolve the situation. Your attention is what kids most want, so to get this attention sometimes children will behave badly. The best way to encourage good behavior in children is to pay attention when they are behaving well and to take your attention from them when they are behaving badly. This is completely counter-intuitive for us and can be a difficult habit to cultivate. But once you get used to it, it will become easier and easier.

A great way to do this is to play with your child when he is quiet in his corner and praise him when he obeys you the first time you speak.

Understand The Stage Of Development

This tip is easy to understand. Each child has a behavior; however, you cannot require a child of three to act as the same as a child who is ten. That is, do not try to go to a three-hour lunch with your little boy hoping he will be quiet for the whole lunch. Do not want a two-year-old child not to put everything in his mouth. Each age has a phase, and it is no use wanting to demand different behavior from a child.

Have Appropriate Expectations

This is a continuation of the above tip. Parents have high expectations. This is not wrong when expectations are possible. For example, do not expect a tired child to behave well, or a one-month-old baby to sleep through the night.

Create Structure and Routine

A child with a structured routine tends to behave better. They already know what to expect and are used to it. A child with a routine feels safe and thus lives more calmly. A child without a routine has a sense of insecurity that will disrupt much in the time to educate and encourage good behavior.

Uses Disciplinary Strategies

Rather than humiliating or beating children, there are positive disciplinary strategies that teach, set boundaries, and encourage good behavior in children. Some of these are: give options, put somewhere to think, talk, give affection and a system of rewards (reward can be a simple compliment, it does not have to be gifts or food).

Understand That The Bad Behavior Worked So Far

If throwing tantrums and disobeying worked for him to get your attention so far, changing this behavior will take time. He will have to realize and understand that you will no longer pay attention to him when he behaves badly, but when he behaves well.

Instilling good behavior practices in young children is a must for any responsible parent, but sometimes it can also be quite complicated and laborious. However, beginning to instill this type of behavior as early as possible will help build a good foundation for the child's behavior and attitudes in the future. It is necessary to be aware that in the first years of life the children are like "sponges" and results will be better if you begin to show them early and direct them to appropriate behaviors of life in society.

Here are some more ideas to help parents with the task of encouraging good behavior in their children.

Models To Follow

Children tend to mirror the behaviors of parents and those with whom they coexist more closely. Therefore, be careful about your behaviors and language used when the child is around to avoid misunderstanding ideas and misconceptions about how you should behave towards others. This includes talking properly and behaving politely to both your partner and family, as well as to the child. Try to avoid loud, unstructured arguments when the child is around. We do not mean you can't disagree with your spouse, because the child must also be aware that these exist. But try to have the arguments always controlled and civil around children.

Be Firm

Parents should be affectionate, but still adamant about instilling discipline in their children. It is important that the child knows how to respect his parents, even when he does not have what he wants. Understanding when to say "no" at the right times is an important step in your education.

Positive Body Language

Your body language has a huge impact when you are trying to instill a particular behavior in children. Given the height of the child, a parent standing while correcting the errors and applying discipline is often viewed as authoritative. It is advisable to place yourself at the same level as the child's eyes. Sit next to the child while talking to them and always maintain eye contact.

Establishing Limits

It is fundamental to establish limits, rules, and consequences for unwanted behavior. Increase limits on children to be able to distinguish right from wrong. They need to know what is not acceptable and clear reasons that make it wrong so that there is no doubt in the child's mind about the behavior to adopt.

You started tracking your child's progress long before he left the warmth of your belly: in the tenth week, the heart began beating; on the 24th week, his hearing developed and listened to your voice; in the 30th week, he began to prepare for childbirth. Now that he or she is in your arms, you're still eager to keep up with all the signs of your little one's development and worries that he might be left behind. Nonsense! Excessive worry will not help at all, so take your foot off the accelerator and enjoy each phase. Your child will realize all the fundamental achievements of maturity. He will learn to walk, talk, potty, and when you least expect it, you will be riding a bicycle alone (and no training wheels!). He will do all only in his time.

Stop taking developmental milestones so seriously. For example, your 7-month-old son will be able to sit alone and at age 3 will be able to ride a tricycle. Consider what is expected for each age just for reference. The best thing to do is to set aside the checklist of the abilities your child needs to develop and play together a lot. There is no better way to connect with and develop your child than through playtime.

To help you even further in realizing the goals mentioned above or processes, I would like to mention some tips here that stimulate a child's intellectual, motor, social, and emotional development:

Rainbow

The baby starts noticing colors at around 3 months of age when the vision is no longer so blurry. That is why, at this age, the idea is to stimulate with strong colors, which can be in toys or mobile in the crib. Babies also love contrast: you can see that stripes are not missing in children's toys. At about a year and a half, your child will begin to notice the difference between one color and another, even if he does not know the color's name. So, start saying: "Let's play with that blue ball" or "Take the red tomato from the salad." This way colors become part of their day to day life.

Books

The role of parents is fundamental for children to learn to love reading and to make books a pleasure, rather than an obligation. According to the latest edition of the Portraits of Reading survey in Brazil, for 43% of readers, the mother was the main influence for developing the desire for reading, and for 17%, the father was the one who played the role. From the third month of your child's life, you can use plastic books in the bath. From the sixth, when the baby can already carry objects to the mouth with his hands, leave cloth books in the cradle - in addition to being able to bite them, he will not be able to rip the pages! At all ages, talk about the cover, the pictures, the colors and let the child turn the pages.

Memory

Memory is a form of storing knowledge and must be permeated by a context. Start by helping your child memorize words by showing a represented object. If you are walking on the street and crossing a bicycle, point and say, "Look, son, a bicycle." This is how he will build associations. From the first year, he will say a few words and try to repeat the names of what you show. But it is from the age of 2 that the ability to retain information increases.

Creating

Create characters and a dream of fantastic worlds. All of this is important in developing the creativity of little ones; it also contributes to problem-solving. To make the narrative more exciting, how about testing the improvisational ability of the two of you? Separate figures from objects, landscapes, colors, foods, and animals – they can be drawn or cut from magazines. While one narrates, the other can select images that portray elements that should be included in the narrative. The challenge is to be able to fit them together so that the narrative continues to make sense. By age 7, as the child is already literate, you can help him record your adventures in small booklets.

Always Ask

When picking up your child from school, you say, "How was your day?" And he says, "Cool." It was not exactly what you wanted to hear, right? To avoid generic responses, develop the questions so that the child needs to express what he thinks and justify his response. Ask: "What did you enjoy most today?" And he will be forced to develop more elaborate reasoning, requiring him to work linguistic and logical skills. At 3 years old, he can already relate experiences he went through and say whether those were good or bad. At 4, you can ask for details, descriptions, and names of colleagues who were with him.

Blessed Doubt

"Why does a dog not eat pizza?" "Was Grandma Ever a Child?" Although child questioning can make adults uncomfortable or embarrassed, these are essential for understanding the child's world. It is the process of distinguishing between real and imaginary (which occurs around the age of 4) and the construction of relations between known elements. That's why the "why questions" are so important in the child's development process. Even if you do not know how to respond to everything your child asks, show that his or her concern is relevant, and recognize when you do not know the answer.

Play, Clean, Play

As your child plays, insist that he engage in one game at a time, to build concentration. "Do you not want to play bowling anymore?" From age 2, your child can help clean up the toy he was using, before picking up a new one, so he also develops the sense of organization.

Belly-Down

Your child begins to strengthen the body between the first and the sixth month. Because thick motor development (involving the activities of large muscles such as sitting and walking) occurs in the head to toe direction, the first step is to strengthen the neck muscles. Beginning the first month, give your child at least two periods a day supported belly downtime on a flat and firm surface. In this way, the baby can lean securely and lift his head. At 6 months, he will start to sit alone. Arrange several cushions around him to help him get stronger.

Clap, Clap, Tum, Tum

One of the best ways to develop motor coordination is to teach rhythm to your child. To do this, just use your hands. From the seventh month, clap with him to the sounds of your favorite songs, interspersing slow songs with other accelerated songs, so he can see the difference. You will see that your baby will be able to hit his little hands.

Everything Fits

From the age of 7 months, the baby begins to hold objects; in about a year and a half, he will begin to put pieces together. Besides being a good exercise for coordination, the child will learn which part will fit within the other. For your child to enjoy and learn from this, he can play with pots and plastic mugs while you prepare lunch. From the age of two and a half, also offer small puzzles (about six pieces).

Step By Step

Climbing stairs is a great exercise to develop agility and coarse motor coordination, as well as assisting to strengthen muscles. At 1 year of age, the child can already perform the activity, but only by placing both feet on the same step, one at a time. With growth, he will gain strength and balance until by age 3, he will probably rise by placing one foot on each step alternately. Even at this stage, it is important that he be accompanied by an adult to avoid accidents.

Bonding & Trust

Establishing relationships of trust is important for the development of the child. The first people he does it with are the parents. For this, one factor is essential: never lie. If the child goes to the doctor to take a vaccine, do not even think about saying that you are just going for a walk. If he asks if the injection will hurt, be honest and say it will, yes, but it will pass. The experts are all in agreement: explain everything. Tell him he's going to get wet, it's going to hurt, he's going to be cold, so he knows what to expect and learns to trust what you say.

Congratulate your child when he is good at something, encouraging him to continue. If scolding is necessary, pay close attention to how to do it. Saying "what you did was naughty" is quite different from saying "you are naughty!" Do not let the child think that the criticized trait is part of his personality, so he will not incorporate this trait into his self-image.

Chapter 3: Behavior Management Tips & Tools

We've made a list of tips that will help you deal with issues that influence children's behavior.

1 - Fights can be difficult for a child. It's even worse if this conflict happened between the parents. Understand the importance of maintaining a harmonious home where feelings are accepted and discussed without judgment. Disregarding a situation that has been recognized by your child, can be harmful to their emotional development. If your child understands an argument or feels the tension in your home, explain that yes, his feelings are valid but that he is safe and loved.

2 - Letting your child make decisions and letting him dream about the future without fear will help him be a happier and more confident child. Allow self-expression and applaud your child's desires. Reinforce and "I can do it!" attitude.

3 - Getting your child to know, appreciate, and respect other cultures is not only a cool thing to do, it can help them in the future. Understanding other ways of living will allow them to be more approachable and respectful, allowing for better relationships and success.

4 - Helping your child to feel loved and special, in addition to his siblings, can shape his identity and present him with a healthy sense of self-esteem in the present and future. Everyone needs to believe in themselves!

5 - Children lie and do not always understand the gravity of a lie. Understanding where they are in development is necessary here. Talking about what harm lies can cause is essential in developing their grasp on how all the world works.

6 - Teaching gratitude to your child creates a happier child and can be fun. People love good news, especially children. What's better than having something to be grateful for? Teach your children to be grateful for the small things such as the weather, their toys and clothes, the fun they have at the park, or even the hug they receive. There will always be something to be grateful for, and this way of thinking can change their world for the better.

7 - Humor is very important in the individual and social development of your child. Laughing is healthy. Being able to see the humor in situations can help build personality.

8 - Children are surrounded by issues that can cause anxiety and fear. Fear of the unknown is fear of most everything for young children, not to mention the size difference for a child in an adult

world. Explore with your child and teach them to feel capable and safe.

9 - You may have heard about "The Terrible Two's". Be aware of what to expect from the tantrum phase. Most parents would agree that the terrible two's is referring to 2 and 3-year-olds. Remember to practice patience and understanding. Children at this stage are ready to communicate and get around on their own, and we need to convey to them that they are still learning. Make learning fun by giving them jobs as a helper with tasks you would normally do alone.

10 - Each of a child's actions has a meaning, but it is not always clear what it means. Pay close attention to the context of your child's behaviors, and you will understand what each behavior of your child means.

11 - This may seem like nothing to you, but for your child, it can mean a lot: Respect your child's growing emotional skills. Their knowledge of the world is rapidly expanding and can become overwhelming. Never embarrass a child for feeling a certain way.

12 - It is normal for some children to feel uncomfortable in new situations. Giving them the rundown before you leave the house allows them to know what to expect and it can help with confidence.

Be Aware Of The Difficulties Of The Child

According to experts, persistent difficulties in performing tasks can indicate signs of hearing problems, vision or hyperactivity, and should be analyzed before raising the conclusion.

Certain behaviors may direct parents to find out if the child suffers from these disorders. It's important to pay attention to troubles your child may have and discuss them with your doctor regularly. All children develop differently, so don't jump to conclusions on your own.

Behavior Modification Techniques

The great number of learning studies carried out in the behavioral field (especially by B. F. Skinner on) allowed the delineation of an intervention methodology named *Applied Behavior Analysis (ABA)* and *behavior modification*. This technical-scientific approach aim to preventing, managing and solving children's behavioral problems. In this context, "behavior" refers to actions and abilities.

Below, I will explain to you the main evaluation strategies and educational intervention. Specifically, I will specifically focus on:
- procedures for proper observation of children's abilities and difficulties (behavioral assessment).

- I will focus on strategies to enhance positive behaviors and on strategies to decrease problematic behavior.

Skills And Behavior Assessment

- Consider the level of development of the child a precise evaluation of his abilities both in the cognitive and behavioral field. To help you: download the free developmental checklist at the beginning of this book.
- Consider the strength and weak points of your child to organize suitable learning situations.
- A functional assessment aimed at understanding the motivations behind the behaviors. Check if there were any changes in the child's family life (for example, the birth of a brother), or if your child has slept enough and is in good health. Sometimes challenging behavior is the first sign to indicate that the child is not well.

Teaching Skills To Children: Strategies

As already stated, behavioral management involves educational work aimed at acquiring and consolidating various functional skills and competences. The main strategies used to acquire and consolidating skills and abilities in children are:

- Prompting and fading
- Modeling
- Shaping
- Chaining
- Reinforcement

Prompting And Fading

The technique is to provide the child with one or more stimuli in the form of instructions (Prompts), to achieve the desired skill. Prompts are usually obvious and are proposed at the exact moment the performance should occur. These can be divided into:

- Verbal suggestions
- Gestural indications
- Physical guidance

Depending on your child's level, they can be provided in the form of vocal verbal instructions (such as explaining, telling, etc.) and non-verbal (such as written, images, etc.). These prompts must necessarily be reduced or modified (Fading) to allow the definitive integration of the ability in the behavioral repertoire of your child.

Modeling

Much of our learning is based on imitation. Much of what we have learned in our lives, we have learned from observing other people. In these cases, other people are the model for our behavior. The ability to imitate is, therefore, a requirement of great importance for human beings. The modeling technique consists in the proposal of learning experiences through the observation of the behavior of the subject that acts as a model.

The modeling technique is used when a parent intends to teach his child, through imitation, certain new behavior that he is unable to implement quickly through other modalities. This is a technique that allows reaching important goals at the level of behavior, but, above all at the relational level. It allows, in fact, to adapt the adult's expectations to achievable goals, avoiding making negative feelings on the child such as frustration, and establishing a virtuous spiral of reciprocal reinforcements: the adult reinforces the child for small improvements and such improvements reinforce the adult in return.

Shaping

In practice, with this technique, we will repeatedly reinforce those behaviors that, although far from the targeted behavior, progressively approach the goal.

B.F. Skinner describes shaping with the analogy, operant conditioning is compared to a ceramist who shapes a piece of clay. The ceramist's product will have a specific shape but we will not be able to find the precise moment in which this form will appear. Likewise, is a certain response from a child is not something that appears suddenly but the result of an ongoing process of formation.

Reinforcement must, therefore, be provided initially to behaviors that are relatively easy for the subject, and then reinforce those that are increasingly closer to the target behavior. To do this we need to break down the final objective into small sub-goals. In this way, we will reduce the expectation of the child. Gently pushing to his small improvements every time, until reaching the final goal.

Chaining

Chaining or step by step is a strategy used for teaching complex skills. When teaching complex skills such as personal autonomy like dressing, washing hands, brushing teeth, you need to split the tasks into small, separate steps to facilitate learning. When you use chaining, the first step is to prepare and complete a task analysis, identifying all the smallest teachable units of behavior that constitute a behavioral chain.

Task analysis to teach your child how to brush his or her teeth might look like this:

- Take the toothbrush

- Squeeze a small amount of toothpaste onto the toothbrush
- Wet the toothbrush under the tap
- Brush the teeth

There are two procedures for teaching a chain of behaviors: forward chaining and backward chaining. Using forward chaining, the behavior is taught in its natural order. Every single phase of the sequence is taught and reinforced once the entire sequence is completed correctly. Using backward chaining, all behaviors identified in the activity analysis are initially completed by the adult, except for the final behavior of the chain. Then it is the turn of the second last step and so on. An advantage of backward chaining is that the child has the feeling of having successfully completed a task before mastering the entire procedure. This gives to him confidence and motivates him to continue his efforts.

Reinforcement

Reinforcement is the most important and widely applied principle of behavioral analysis and regulates most of our daily activities. Reinforcement can be defined as a consequence that strengthens a given behavior with the chance that it happening again in the future.

Reinforcements can be of two different types: positive and negative. When it comes to behavior, positive and negative do not mean good or bad.

They simply must be intended as algebraic signs that is the add and subtract. The positive reinforcement increases the probability that behavior is repeated thanks to the positive effect that this provides. For example, a child is learning to read, the mother is close to him and when the child reads correctly, she tells him: "good" (positive reinforcement); reading acquires a positive value for the child because for him it is a source of attention from the mother. Negative reinforcement also increases the probability that a behavior will be repeated because this removes a certain negative effect. For example, the child cries because she's hungry her mother rushes to feed her, in similar situations, when the child will be hungry, she will cry again to get her mother's attention. Negative reinforcement is not punishment. Punishment does not lead to the extinction of behavior but it will make it less likely to occur in the future.

In punishment, there is no learning. Certain behavior is inhibited, blocked (usually momentarily) without learning new behaviors. In reinforcement instead, both positive and negative, there is learning because in the case of positive reinforcement we learn a new behavior that has positive effects, in the case of negative reinforcement you learn a new behavior that is useful to stop something negative.

How to effectively use reinforcement when working to teach new behaviors?

- Reinforcements should be customized based on child preferences: observe the child's interests and motivation to determine which reinforcements are best.
- Reinforcement should be immediate: this means that the reinforcement should be delivered immediately after the desired behavior appears.
- Reinforcement must also be associated with behavior: in other words, the level of reinforcement must adapt to behavior.
- You associate tangible reinforcements to social reinforcements: sometimes it is important to combine praise with rewards.
- Continuous reinforcement and intermittent reinforcement: it is important to constantly decrease the number of reinforcements given over time.

Reinforcement is an important principle that determines an actual change in behavior. It is used in all ABA programs but it is also something that happens naturally in your everyday life. Think about your days and your life: you will realize that almost everything is driven by the principle of reinforcement and that all our behavior is encouraged or not by the response we get.
Below we will explain through simple examples four proven behaviors modification techniques.

Behavioral Intervention Techniques

Parent's behavioral intervention techniques are usually based on the consequences of a child's behavior. Those interventions attempt to change behavior through the application of positive or negative consequences. Positive and negative consequences increase or decrease the frequency, intensity and duration of a given behavior, they are used as rewards or sanctions.

When applied correctly, positive consequences can be very effective in modifying children's behavior. Experience suggests that whenever positive consequences are immediate, regular and modified in order to avoid a certain habit, children can reach good results. The first step that parents have to do to intervene with positive consequences, is to observe the child's actions in order to determine which consequences can be truly reinforcing for the child, that is, which prizes, situations or actions are effective to strengthen the desired behavior.

The use of negative consequences for the child can be carried out through some techniques including planned ignoring, the cost of answer and time-out. Since the negative consequences are effective regulators of human behavior, these must be applied adequately and safely in a controlled environment.

Time-Out

The time-out can be used in two ways. One of these is the typical reaction to unwanted behaviors: "go to your room for five minutes" or "sit for five minutes in punishment." This type of time-out will be seen by the child as a negative conclusion or punishment. Probably, the most effective approach is to think at time-out as a pause to the child's poor behavior and not as a punishment, a short period of time that allows the child and the parent to have a few minutes to distance themselves from negative behaviors, in order to process them and calm down.

What happens after the time-out is very important! Some believe that, after a time-out and before anything else, the child has to come back and apologize. Others instead conceive time-out as time spent moving away from negative behavior and then being able to rejoin the family without the embarrassment of having to apologize publicly. This second modality is preferable because it allows the child to reconnect more naturally to the activity interrupted and, on the other hand, avoids the emotional problems linked to having to apologize.

Cost Of Response

This technique is used to remove something pleasant from the child. In other words, fines or penalties will be applied when negative behavior occurs. We use the cost of response to avoid providing the child with feedback to inappropriate behavior in conjunction with positive rewards for appropriate ones. For example, if the child doesn't observe some previously established rules, this procedure involves the loss of a previously earned token or the failure to earn one in the future: "If you don't want to take the coat off the ground, I'll do it but you'll lose a token ".

Token Economy

The establishment of a Token system at home is quite simple. The basic idea is that a child earns tokens every time he achieves an established goal. If the child fails to reach the goal there are no negative consequences; tokens are in fact assigned only to the achievement of the goal or positive behavior. Once a token is earned, this can never be taken away. This allows the child to form a strong link with positive choices. In some cases, as previously mentioned, it is also possible to earn extra credits in order to further incentivize the child's motivation toward positive behaviors. For example, if the child helps to lay the table, as agreed, he earns a token; in addition, if he also offers himself to help to clear up, he could earn additional credit.

To create an effective Token Economy it is necessary to think carefully about the way the table is presented. This needs to contain the description of goals to achieve and relative rewards, also evaluate where to place it in order to make it visible.

Positive Communication

The way we choose to communicate is absolutely important. Rather than say "don't do this or that" we try to communicate our intent using descriptive and positive sentences. "Don't swear" could be expressed as "we use polite language" or "we speak to people respectfully"; "Don't hit" the same way, it could become "we use our hands gently". Try to contain comments and negative reactions. Our interventions, including Token Economy, will be less likely to succeed if we use a punitive tone of voice or aggressive body language. The child may change some of his behaviors for fear of being punished, but this will not help him to grow. Moreover, when the fear is no longer present, the child's behavior will again tend to worsen.

If the child behaves as we expected, reward him by identifying a precise moment and a place. For example, before going to the mall we could say: "If you sit calm and safe while driving, you will receive a reward of two tokens", or "if you sit politely at dinner, at the end of the meal you will get a cake". With these sentences, we have made an accurate and positive description. Always remember to describe the behavior you want.

Chapter 4: Crying & Tantrums

Why Toddlers have Tantrums?

Tantrums are a normal part of a child's development. It is a communication channel chosen by the child to communicate that they are upset or frustrated. Tantrums happen when kids are hungry, tired or uncomfortable; they aren't able to communicate and express what they feel, want or need. There is a neuro-psychological explanation for the tantrums of toddlers. The frontal regions of the brain that determine executive functions (our capacity for planning, self-control, and reasoning) mature later than the other areas of the brain. Thus, it's natural that, in many instances, children have tantrums, because they are not psychologically able to express themselves any other way. One of the most common tantrum reasons is that children cannot handle limits and have great difficulty hearing the word "no".

How To End The Tantrums Of Children?

Leo, now 6 years old, is the son of the publicist Shirley Hilgert, 39, author of the blog Macetes de Mãe. Shirley, who today is also the mother of Caetano, 3, says that when her oldest was 2 years old, there was a situation when he yelled the entire time she was at the cashier's area. While she was embarrassed by the situation, she took a deep breath and put herself in her son's shoes. "He wanted something he could not have; I squatted down and explained to him that he was not going to get it and why. I knew if I gave in at that moment, he would make the same outburst the next time. I stayed firm in the decision."Leo bellowed a little more at the store exit, but, as predicted by his mother, he never repeated the "show."

The Good Side Of The Tantrum (Yes, It Exists)

Does the tactic adopted by Shirley work for everyone? In other words, is there a formula to end the tantrum? The answer is: it depends on the child. A recent study by the universities of Amsterdam and Utrecht (Netherlands) in partnership with the universities of Cardiff and Oxford (UK), analyzed 156 surveys from 20 countries involving 15,000 families with children aged 2 to 10 years who had disruptive tantrums. The researchers detected two groups of techniques most used to deal with the problem: those based on behavior management (combined, for example) and relationship building (dialogue, among others). For children with more frequent disruptive behaviors, the study found that the most effective method is a mixture of the two strategies.

Tears Heal: Why It Is Important To Let Your Child Cry!

What makes empathy an essential point for dealing with so-called "children," especially for strengthening family ties? Within this approach, there are many ways to act. Child psychologist Mayra Gaiato, a master at experimental psychology and behavioral analysis at PUC-SP, suggests three steps: prevention, combined, space and support.

1. Prevention

That's right! For the specialist, parents should warn the child what will happen so that she can "prepare," especially in situations that precede something she does not like or does not want to do. Sometimes you can even use some instruments, like a timer. Does your child cry every time you announce it's time to go home from a party? Before that time, make it clear that you are leaving in five or ten minutes.

In addition, you need to make sure your child's needs, both basic and subtle, such as your feelings and desires. Often, children give indications (by action or facial expression) that he or she is unhappy, before the explosion. These signs may vary from one to the other, of course, but among the most common are: need of sleep, hunger, fatigue, increased aggressiveness, moodiness and impatience. For example, it is no use taking the little one for a walk when what they need is nap time. That will turn into crying for sure! Over time, it will become easier to identify these "triggers."

2. Combined

If the tantrum happens, even if the day is well planned, the second step is negotiation. If your child has a problem when it comes to sitting at the table, the idea in this situation is to lower to the child's height, maintain eye contact and make a combination, such as: Let's have dinner now, and you can play again soon after. "It does not mean giving in and explaining to the child why she cannot do what she wants," says Mayra. Do not confuse empathy with permissiveness.

3. Space and support

If the behavior continues or worsens, the specialist suggests, as a third and final step, that the adult waits for the child to calm down. "You have to wait, give her space and silence. Show her you're around, but cannot talk while she exhibits that behavior. Her brain will understand that she did not get what she wanted and that her "strategy" does not works. Then, when she is calmer, complete the process with "sensory support," as the specialist says, that would be a hug or a kiss, to help soothe the child.

Learning to deal with this behavior that is part of your child's development.

Space For Routine

A child needs routine, so he knows what to expect, and what he can and cannot do. This provides security, and it is the transmission of affection. This holds true for everyday situations such as bathing, dining, and going to school. For this to happen, the whole family needs to be organized. It is like confusing the child with the values of the family: can you imagine how chaotic a home in which right and wrong mix? To keep the rules, it is also essential to make it easier for them to be fulfilled: if you want them to always behave in a public place, they will not let you sit in a crowded restaurant or wait for them to calm down in a bank queue.

Value The No

You already know the importance of saying 'no' for your child to learn to mature and realize that you will not have everything at hand when they ask for something. "Children who are never contradicted end up becoming angry, aggressive, and unhappy adults. After all, the world will not always give an unconditional "yes" if parents have always said that to their child," explains the Child Psychoanalyst Anne Lise Scappaticci. The little word "no" should not be wasted in completely unnecessary situations. When used without moderation, the word "no" can lose strength and invite disobedience.

Act On Punishment

It is of no use to punish children under 2 years of age. They are not mature enough to realize that they have done something wrong. For example, if your child throws a toy on the floor or against someone and you take the toy, that's a punishment for her. When the child is older, it is worth removing something important for the child, like the classic "No TV". Punishments, when properly applied, serve the sense of justice that all children have. The lack of punishment, on the contrary, disorientates them. A quiet, serious look at a child is a particularly effective kind of punishment. The purpose of punishment is to make the child think.

To be educative, the child needs to understand the relationship between what he did and the consequence. The punishment must happen at the same time because children have an immediate vision: they have not yet learned to think in the long run. That is, after some time, they do not know why they are being punished, they forgot the original offense.

We are not talking about spanking, pinching or slapping. That is unnecessary.

Tantrums usually occur around the age of two, which is when children leave the baby stage and gradually begin to perceive themselves as an individual with their own opinions. Children at this age, due to the lack of maturity, express themselves through the tantrum to show their desires and feelings.

How You Deal With The Tantrums

Children learn much by examples. The best way is to have self-control during small tantrums. If we deal with the tantrums of children with aggression or punishment, they will learn that aggression is acceptable. It is important for parents to control their own feelings when their child gets out of control.

The biggest mistake that parents do at the time of tantrums is to do the will of the child to prevent him from continuing to scream or cry. Although unpleasant and embarrassing in many situations, do not give in.

When parents make a decision, and they go back as a result of the child's tantrum, the child will begin to understand that one can always make a temper tantrum and at some point, the parents will give in.

But Then, What To Do?

At this point, I should stress the importance of parents helping their children deal with frustration. Only this will grow strong and fearless adults.

Of the many demands that exist when tending to children, the difficulty they have in dealing with the "no" is undoubtedly the greatest. These are children who grow up with great difficulty tolerating frustration. They do not know how to cope with that emotion. They do not know how to accept it. And, above all, they despair! Imposing limits, lovingly, is the best way.

What Do Mothers Have To Say?

Who has not had a situation when their child had public tantrums? Here is an excerpt from the words of a mother facing some similar issues. "In these last months, he has been very silly and stupid when he hears to 'no' from us. He crouches on the floor, cries, sometimes hit us, or beats himself (in the head). At dawn, for example, if I do not breastfeed at the time he wants, he screams a lot, kicks me and does not listen to me at all," explains the mother.

She knows that this phase is complicated, requires patience and lots of conversation, but sometimes the situation is beyond her control. "I often lose my temper and talk a bit louder, but it's not the right way to deal with it. Sometimes I ignore or try to distract him with other things, like toys, drawings, painting. I think it's just a phase that is known as "Terrible Two's," which many mothers go through during this same age group."

Positive Discipline

Let's take another example to understand: Dandara Brito (mother), 27, João Miguel's(child), now 2 years and 3 months old. Dandara began to use positive discipline at home, a pedagogical approach based on mutual respect and cooperation, which aims to help parents in their child's education.

Positive discipline is considered a compromise between the rigid and permissive way of educating the little ones, giving them limits, but wherever possible, with choices. It is a program based on the studies of two Austrian psychologists, Alfred Adler, and Rudolf Dreikurs, from the beginning of the last century.

Positive discipline (a way of educating that has been gaining more and more acceptance), aims to encourage children and adolescents to become responsible, respectful, resilient and provides resources to solve problems throughout life.

"João's tantrums began to happen at 1 year and 8 months. Usually, it occurs when he wants to do something not allowed or when he has a tiring day. He screams a lot, cries; sometimes he throws himself on the floor, "she explains.

Dandara points out that she seeks to validate her son's feelings and understand what he wants to convey at that moment.

"It's a phase where they are maturing their emotions and usually cannot deal with them. I always try to search, and the best way I can handle these moments without being permissive but being kind. And I try to apply positive discipline and non-violent education", she says. Around the age of two, the parents are faced with a child full of desire and ready to open the shout when being contradicted. There are days when he only eats food if it is on the plate. In others, they do not want to eat. Hence, he asks to watch TV or use the iPad, but at bedtime. And when he hears "no" from his parents, he starts beating and throwing toys, cries desperately and throws himself on the floor. Later, he is reluctant to enter the bath, and when he enters, he is reluctant to leave.

Such situations become routine in the lives of parents of children approaching two years of age when the phase dubbed "babies' adolescence" begins.

And, behold, these parents, who were getting used to a baby who accepted almost everything passively, are surprised by a child full of will and ready to scream when being contradicted. The good news is that this is not only normal but a crucial part of child development. And learning from child experiences at that age will help shape the way he deals with his feelings in adulthood. The second good news is that there are many clever ways to deal with these behaviors as long as parents are armed with strategies and patience.

BBC News talked to four child behavior experts to learn about the importance of this phase around the age of 2 to 4 years in development and raised ten practical tips to guide parents in day-to-day situations.

What Happens Around The Age Of Two?

"It's a phase where the child makes incredible discoveries and gains tremendous ability to interact, but the areas of self-regulation in his brain have not yet developed," explains Ross Thompson, a professor in the Department of Psychology at the University of California, Davis and president of council of the organization Zero to Three, dedicated to this age group.

"The most important thing is for parents to understand that this child is simply unable to control their emotions. This understanding will help them see it more constructively, rather than think it is challenging their authority. Telling a child to calm down will not work at this age. It is up to the adult to help her put her feelings into words and manage them. "

"The child begins to realize that it is not an extension of the parents, but a person with desires. And to these new desires there is intense frustration, accompanied by cries and cries," says educator parental Elisama Santos.

Children at this age are dying to use their newfound autonomy. This maturation of emotional control in the brain lasts until the early 20s, but the most critical phase of this "babyhood" usually goes away by 4 years, when children increase their repertoire to express themselves and understand the world. Until then, if parents get carried away by anger and become punitive, situations tend to get out of control. If instead they act calmly, empathically, and offer strategies for this child, this one will learn tools to deal with their emotions - something that will help them through adulthood.

When The Child Strikes

When contradicted, many children from a year and a half, beat up on parents or caregivers. Unable to express their frustration in words or to calm down on their own, they resort to physical reactions. "stop beating, you're grounded!" - The child will become more nervous and will not know what to do with their feelings. Instead, explain to the child what he is feeling and giving tools for him to overflow. "I know you're upset, but we do not eat sweets at this time of day." "When you're sad, hit this drum rather than beating people," or "bite this toy instead of biting Mom, "for example.

Repeating this several times, the tendency is for the child to begin to understand their feelings and the resources to manage them. A hug helps calm down in tantrum moments.

Elisama Santos gives similar tips: teach the child to clap or roar like a lion when they need to release the energy of anger.

"I also suggest talking in a tone of curiosity: 'Did you see that your little hand hit me? You're the boss of the little hand, you take care of it.'"

"This is difficult in a culture that blames parents when kids are making tantrums," she says. "(But) remember that your child is not purposely trying to humiliate you - he simply cannot handle the situation. Your job is not to punish him, but to empathize, validate his emotions, guide him, and keep him safe. Let people think what they want. "

Help the child express in words what she is feeling (frustration, anger, irritation) and offer her arms and arms - even if she does not say, 'Mom is here when you want a hug.' And let her cry, making sure she's in a safe space if she's floundering.

Changing the environment, looking at the sky, taking a turn, and taking the focus off the tantrum motif often helps to "turn off the pump." But experiencing the sadness of frustration is part of the (difficult) process of growing up. Cure heals and is a tool to calm down. Learning to recognize feelings and deal with frustration is a process that begins at this age.

The Limits

Keeping calm does not mean giving in to the child's desires, which would give her a counterproductive message: hereupon "if I make a tantrum, I will get what I want." If you give in, you will not strengthen the muscle of resilience or teach the child to deal with frustration, something essential for adulthood. The way is not to be permissive, to say 'no' when necessary and to welcome the frustration that comes from that.

Children are testing their power and their choices, and if the father does not stick to the limit he has set, the behavior will continue, and it is necessary to impose time limits on the TV or tablets. If the child does not want to put on his seat belt, put it on, be impassive, and move on. He will gradually realize that even if he does not cooperate, the belt will be put on anyway.

Do Not See Acts As Manipulation

For children so small and in times of stress, little use is made of asking "why did you knock?" or start big discussions - they are too small to understand, and the tendency is only to increase tantrums. Children are provocative; they will say, 'I hate you,' they will beat you. If we see this as manipulation - while they are typical behaviors of that age - we still tend to react angrily.

Providing A Chance For The Child To Choose

To prevent long-lasting battles and the child from taking control of the family routine - at meals, at the time of dressing, when leaving, give acceptable choices to children, who are dying to exercise their newfound autonomy. The trick is always to give two choices to children and set limits. For example, in the case of toys scattered around the floor of the house, you have two great ones: If you do not clean up, Mom or Dad will have to spend time doing it, so we'll not have a book to read at bedtime.

The idea is to give consequences to the choices of the children, but appropriate to the situation.

Instead Of 'No,' Positive Reinforcement

To Elishama Santos, children of this age say "no" to (almost) everything because they are used to hearing a lot of "no's" from parents - who, although well-intentioned to protect children, can use a more efficient strategy: positive reinforcement.

It's no use saying that she should not put her hand in the socket, because what she's going to fix is just the socket. It's better to give instructions on what she should do rather than what she shouldn't.

Playing More - Choosing Battles

Turning everyday activities into jokes helps relieve stress in boring tasks, says the parent educator. If you use a robot voice or make tinsel to wear or brush children's teeth, it will take that phase more lightly and easily. Avoid getting into all the (exhausting) battles with children. If it does not interfere with the functioning of the family and does not hurt anyone, I recommend leaving it there - for example, if your child decides to leave the house with a shirt that does not fit with the pants.

Plan To Prevent Tantrum

Identify patterns of behavior to prevent tantrums: for example, changing the bath or bath time. And if you know what caused the tantrum of the previous day, you can try to stop it today with conversations. 'Remember that yesterday was a very difficult time for bathing?'.

Is 'Educational' Slap Going To Help?

Experts advised by BBC News - whether to teach limits or to get the child out of dangerous situations - will not help the educational process so crucial at this stage. Violence tends to make children angrier and more challenging, and parents more punitive - in a vicious cycle. The same goes for verbal assaults. The child will only find that it is not loved enough - and it is very bad to spend this phase of life finding it.

Lost control? It has salvation

Sometimes the parents themselves get carried away by the situation, even if they do not want to see each other screaming or losing their patience with their children. It may be a great time to teach children to take responsibility for their actions.

If the situation allows, it is also possible to "take a break" by saying 'Mom will take a moment to think' this is a possible way out. It gives you a moment to breathe and to elaborate on what choices you will offer your children. And parents can benefit from having another adult around whom they can turn to when they are about to lose their temper - and ask them to take the lead. Finally, experts point out that the tips given above will have to be repeated a few times until they are internalized by such small children. That is, prepare your patience.
In the beginning, it takes time and effort for parents to manage their own reactions. But the payoff is huge: it will come in the form of more self-control of children, more cooperation in daily tasks and more positive cycles of interaction.

Chapter 5: Common Behavior Concerns

As they grow, all children are likely to go through challenging situations that cause worrisome thoughts. The role of parents is not necessarily to eliminate anxiety but to help control it. Prothero, a psychologist who specializes in childhood anxiety disorders, said that regardless of whether a child was diagnosed with anxiety or not, the way parents can help does not change. "We have seen many children referred for treatment in the last five years, and this seems to be increasing," the therapist told The Huffington Post UK. Parents can really do a lot at home to help a child who is suffering from anxiety.

If you notice that your child suffers from anxiety, you can be sure that you are not alone. Parents should only worry if they notice that their child's anxiety is having a significant effect on school or their relationships. Many children do not know what they feel when they are anxious, and this can be very scary and oppressive.

Identifying Signs of Anxiety in Your Child

I'll mention some examples where a mother connected the dots of some of the problems their child was suffering from, for example: bed-time problems, with the potential anxiety they might be suffering from through open, polite conversations and understanding.

"My son is almost 8 years old, and the first time I noticed his anxiety he was 4 1/2 years old," said Jordan Martin, 35, whose son is anxious before going to school. "I had to take him to school despite signs of anxiety, which were unusual [in his personality]: crying, shaking and holding his belly," said the mother. "I would drop him off at school and cry when I got home... It was very important to be consistent for him to go to school, but I felt terrible."

Martin cited as other signs of anxiety the child's fear of bed-time; he said that "bad things" could happen. "He cared about silly things like his school backpack not being at home, anything related to change," he added.

Salma Shah, whose 5-year-old daughter has anxious thoughts, often said that the behavior has been constant since she was a baby. "As a baby, I remember her turning her back on all the other babies and turning to me, distracting me by pointing at things," Shah explained.

"One of the main symptoms I noticed when she grew up was her attachment. If she had a 'playdate,' she would always be by my side and never spoke voluntarily to people, not even to family members with whom she had always had contact. "

Natasha Jones, 35, said the anxiety of Ella, her 7-year-old daughter, came when she was saddened to think about illness and death in the family. This was reinforced the first time she saw Harry Potter and Cinderella. The films sparked concern about death and the possibility of losing parents. "She was constantly worried if she was alone at home or with another family member," Jones explained. "The problem got worse if I was not at home. It affected her concentration on things like homework or playing, and she became very sensitive before bed, with frequent stomach pain."

Now, how to help control a child's anxiety?

1. Divide Situations Into Small Portions

When a child is feeling anxious about a scenario, it is tempting to help her avoid it. But with that, he will never develop confidence. Instead, help them break up the situation they are having trouble with into small pieces and make lots of compliments with rewards as they tackle each 'piece' before moving to the next level.

For example, if a child is socially anxious, encourage him to attend small meetings and allow him to get used to it before attempting a slightly larger party.

2. Use Relaxation Techniques

Martin creates a "safe place" for the son, where he can feel protected and calm before going to bed. She talks to him using relaxation techniques, such as a soft tone and positive phrases.

The words parents can say during this relaxation should be the most appropriate for the child's needs. I use the first person, which works well, for example: 'Repeat in your mind:' I'm safe, I'm home wherever I am, it's okay.' A soft tone, with a light touch on the shoulder or chest, works well. And Martin is a great example of the same.

Be careful not to use negative words, so instead of saying, 'Do not be scared,' say something like: 'You're safe, all is calm, and all is well.'

3. Teach Breathing Techniques

Breathing, in general, helps anyone who is feeling anxious to draw attention to the action of breathing and not to the cause of worry. Controlling this can create a sense of calm and prevent future anxiety attacks. Martin said he uses these techniques to calm his son. "I use the technique of inhaling through the nose counting to four and then exhaling through the nose counting to four," he said.

The goal is for children to regain control over their emotions; so if they face a 'scary' or 'uncomfortable' situation, they can resort to safe and effective strategies, such as the powers of a superhero.

4. Stimulate A 'Happy Thought'

Martin says he tries to tell his son a statement positive every night before he goes to sleep and every morning before he goes to school - which is when he feels more anxious. "He now asks for this specifically," he said. "I think he feels safe and supported, knowing he can focus on this when he goes to sleep or on the way to school. My husband was the one who started with the 'happy thought.' My son asks, 'What is my happy thought?' ".

Encourage the children to choose their own happy memory because it is their mind, and only they can know what animates their spirit.

5. Prepare For Anxiety-Provoking Situations

"We have come to places or parties early, so my daughter has not to walk among a lot of people, "Shah said, explaining that the daughter feels anxious in social situations. She said that preparing for possible anxiety situations in advance allows the daughter to deal better with them. "She responds kindly to kindness," she added. "We also highly commend her when she actually attends a party or event to reinforce her achievement."

6. Over time, Expose Your Child to Different Circumstances

Shah said parents should never worry about the possible embarrassment of the child being "too attached." They should focus more on building trust in their children. Do not push them too hard. But kindly, over time, expose them to different circumstances that will get them out of their comfort zone.

7. Do Not Get Angry, Work As A Team

"We try to be understanding and recognize my daughter's problems," explained Jones. "We've done a lot of research to try out techniques that would suit Ella, and one of the best ways to reassure her is to talk to her. Telling her that she's not alone and that other children have the same fears, including me, is comforting. We work as a team, and she knows it will take time for her fear to go away".

8. Create A 'Book Of Worries'

To help children with long-term anxiety, you can create a" worries book," and through that, you can encourage them to see what things make them anxious - their triggers. Just in case they are old enough to do this, have them write their thoughts in a 'book of worries.' Jones said the daughter uses this technique, writing her thoughts into a "box of worries."

9. Talk To Other Parents

For parents who do not know how to help their children deal with anxiety or anxious thoughts, talking with other parents to know their techniques can give ideas. Sometimes the solution is closer than we think.

10. Seek Professional Help If Anxiety Persists

If anxiety does not improve over two or three months or is significantly affecting your child's ability to socialize or go to school, you must seek professional help. Therapists who specialize in children can be consulted privately or through their GP. For example, the British government recommends that children with social anxiety have 8-12 sessions of cognitive-behavioral therapy.

Children are anxious by nature. In the car, they ask every five minutes how much time is left to complete the trip. At school, they may experience belly pain on test days. At home, they hang around the kitchen until dinner is served. The willingness to anticipate situations and the excitement of what is to come is part of child development - but to a limit. When they start to generate suffering and get in the way of everyday life, it can be a sign of a bigger problem.

According to the American Association of Anxiety Disorders, between 9% and 15% of the population aged five to 16 suffers from the disorder, which is characterized by a set of physical reactions, psychological and behavioral that precede a real or imaginary situation.

Carolina Schneider Silva, a psychologist at the Santo Antônio Children's Hospital of Santa Casa de Misericórdia in Porto Alegre, explains that anxiety attacks are disproportionate reactions of children to the stimulus they receive, whatever they will be. In Julia's case, a single line served as a trigger.

Crises can be characterized by a sense of fear and apprehension, marked by a period of tension or discomfort in the face of some event considered dangerous, even if it does not offer real risk. When exaggerated, they may appear in the form of tachycardia, muscle tension, tremors, shortness of breath, fainting, and bowel problems.

Know the Signs, Treatments and Know What to Do

The symptoms of an anxiety disorder may arise suddenly or gradually. Possibly, so they go unnoticed by many parents.

External Stimuli

Childhood is a period of many changes, and the degree of anxiety goes through oscillations as the child grows. Whether at the beginning of the school year, in routine changes or changes in the family environment, external stimuli generate new sensations and emotions.

In this age group, there are two types of anxiety disorder most common: Generalized Anxiety Disorder (GAD) and Anxiety and Separation Disorder (ASD). Science cannot yet explain why some children develop the problem, but some factors seem fundamental:

- The development of anxiety disorders results from the interaction of multiple factors such as genetic inheritance, the temperament the psychiatrist Gustavo Teixeira, a member of the American Academy of Psychiatry for Childhood and Adolescence and author of books on the same subject.

Experts argue that the picture is also linked to the excess of stimuli that children currently receive. They are subjected to greater social and emotional pressure from both the family and the school, for example.

- It is necessary to know the children and to be alert to changes, be they physical or behavioral. The most common ways of expressing anxiety are through recurring concerns and difficult to control. Together, there may be restlessness, easy tiredness, difficulty concentrating, irritability, and trouble sleeping or staying asleep.

How To Deal With Behavior Disorder In School?

A school brings together students from completely different personalities. There are those quieter students, the more introspective, the communicators, and those who never obey the rules. In the latter case, delivering an activity in the classroom can be quite an exercise in patience. However, you need to be cautious with children because behavioral disorders are much more complex than a simple tantrum.

Early childhood education should be ready to welcome children in general, but it is true that the most questioning, for example, presents a challenge for the educator. When you are faced with a student who has such characteristics, the best way is to be able to deal with each particularity brought to the school environment.

What Are These Behaviors?

Conduct can be diverse and range from challenging questions to physical aggression in extreme cases. However, it is important to point out other behaviors that are related to the disorder referred to in this article: rule violation, disobedience in the classroom, bullying of the child to other colleagues and teachers; cries, impulsive actions, provocations, discussions, and school dropouts.

Preparation

No doubt, there are many parents and teachers who are not prepared to deal with such situations. However, warning children energetically is not a step to be taken, although many do. That's because the little ones can feel challenged and insist on the attitude that motivated the warning made.

How To Deal Then?

The common point of all ways of dealing with behavioral disorders is dialogue. It is important always to establish communication between the child and the adult. Ask the child, the reason for such disobedience and try to have the confidence of the little one. Of course, this is not so simple, but there are ways to reduce the causes of these behaviors:

- Family therapy: support groups that work to develop the relationship between parents and children are a great alternative. In this situation, experts advise parents to establish effective communication with the child and to show them the limits to be placed on the child's behavior.

- Psychological follow-up: the child who presents some behavioral disorder in school can also find ways to improve their relationship and interaction with the environments in which they are. Psychological counseling can mean a very good way for the little one, from the moment therapy can help you get along with everyone around you.

- Multidisciplinary team: nothing more indicated than to act together with a diversified team, that brings together therapists and school teachers in the search for the improvement of the child's behavior.

And The Parents?

Parents and guardians should establish a satisfactory communication with the pedagogical and therapeutic group in order to arrive at an adequate response to the disorder presented.

It is very important that everyone has patience with the child since the child must find trust and authority in adults. To act cautiously does not mean ceasing to impose limits. On the contrary, the limits are indispensable. Adequate follow-up and parental attention are important determinants of behavior disorder.

Chapter 6: Friends & Siblings

Can small children be friends? They can but in their own way. That means you should be prepared to see one bite the other, take the toy without asking ... These are things of the age that need to be understood. In the range of 1 to 3 years, the child is still egocentric, and the question of the possession of objects is very present. Therefore, it is common for them to take a toy from the other's hand and walk.

The little ones are in the famous oral phase, in which they use the mouth as a means of discovering the world. As long as they do not know how to talk, they end up sometimes hitting for no reason, just to get what they want. Of course, if aggressive behavior is too frequent and intense, it requires parental attention. It is not necessary to deprive the one who was caught up in the other's life but to ensure that it happens in the most protected way possible, supervising and separating in case of aggression.

Not infrequently, a more passive child becomes friends with a bossy one. The experts consulted say that the leaderships of the group begin to dawn with 4 or 5 years. When this happens, others become his followers - and make no mistake about their little age: the leader realizes the strength his opinion has over others.

When the teacher identifies this in school, he should use strategies and jokes to dilute this configuration so that roles are reversed in some situations: followers become leaders, and the leader becomes a follower - this can also be done at home by parents. If conflicts arise from the relationship between a leader and a follower, it is recommended that each child should orally expose the other to how he felt and what he did not like. They should listen and try to resolve the situation with each other.

Shy Children

More introverted and shy children may have difficulty making friends. In such cases, parents may approach a class in the playground of the building, for example, and introduce the child, asking if he can play with them. So, next time, he will already have a reference on how to act. You can also invite classmates to attend your home. That way, they will have what to talk about in the room, plus memories of fun times together.

But if the child is never called to any party and seems to be always isolated, the ideal is to do a job with the school to detect why this happens. You can also enroll your child in extracurricular theatre or sports classes that help decrease inhibition. Just do not press it.

If your child is very sociable and makes friends easily, rest easy. Just be aware of whether your child is not acting that way to get attention and can do a little more work with a concentration in the classroom. Point it out that there is time for everything.

Friends – Siblings

Who said siblings could not be good friends? In these cases, one only needs attention if the youngest becomes a" shadow "of the brother and ends up having no personality. Well, then, talk about the importance of having your own attitudes.

There are also cases where siblings have no affinity. Parents should be aware of the context in which the lack of friendship happens and the expectation they have of that relationship. In general, siblings will be friends but often go through situations of jealousy and competition. It may also be that they have different interests, which seems like a lack of friendship, but is related to gender and age. Parents need to look at how they relate to the family (mother, father, and siblings) in order to identify whether they have a strong or superficial bond because the child perceives and tends to have similar behaviors.

Leaving

If the parents look back, they'll remember that some of their own friends walked away for a while and then came back. You have to stay calm and keep in mind that this is a process of building the bond of the child. Another feeling that can arise in such a situation is jealousy. When there is some dependence on friendship, attention is needed. If we identify something negative, that does not benefit both parties. It is necessary to stimulate new friends. The adult should show that the child can discover affinities with several children.

Outside The Party

Make no mistake, this will happen sooner or later, either for financial reasons (it's expensive to invite all the students) or affinity. In these situations, the adult needs to be prepared to face the frustration - of the child and parent. Parents must accept that it is not the end of the world and explain that some people identify more with each other than with others.

The opportunity is ideal for sitting with the child and asking why he thought he was so close to the birthday boy. Sometimes he thinks he's friends with the other, but he's not reciprocated. It is important to have this understanding, that some people give the impression that they are our friends, but they are not.

Colorful Friendship

From the age of 4, children begin to perceive each other better, start comparisons, and have a greater perception of their own body. It is common for situations to arise from one wanting to kiss and embrace the other. Some even talk about dating. This is largely a reflection of what they see daily in the media, that is, an imitation of behavior. When faced with such issues, parents should teach the child that he is able to express affection in various ways - with words, drawings, and jokes together - and to say that he should not kiss another person on the mouth.

My son never wants to leave his friend's house. What to do?

Parents should keep in mind that no matter how friendly they may be, there is no way to force the bond between children. The identity that made them be friends does not necessarily happen among their children. And adults should be prepared even to get upset. If this is your case, it is best to avoid contact between children, especially when there are no others to interact separately. Prefer to date only with adult friends.

The Friend Is a Terror

One way or another you will come across those friends who are a "terror": they make a mess, they mess around the house, they speak profanity ...

The desire to berate the colleague can be enormous. If it is to your child that the message must be given, explain that there are several ways to behave and that the way the other acts do not please you, pointing out how the line has been crossed. The same must be done with swearing. In general, small children do not know what they mean, but if they realize that it causes anxiety in their parents, they can repeat it on purpose, just to manipulate them, just like the tantrum. Therefore, be very calm in explaining that this is not acceptable to say.

Away From Home

Generally, it is at about 4 years that the child starts to go to friends' houses and, from 5, can be prepared to sleep outside the home. Knowing the routine and habits of other families is positive, as it broadens the worldview. It is inevitable, however, that the child will make comparisons and question aspects such as "in so-and-so's house I could stay up late. It is a good chance to teach your child that each family has its own rules - which are not better or worse, just different.

It can happen the opposite also: your son sleeps there and discovers that he does not identify with the style of the family (schedule, food, fear of a pet). Listen and see what he has to say and do not force him back. One option to keep the friendship is to take walks with the colleague elsewhere or let your child visit you for short periods of time.

My Idol

It is common for children to choose a friend as an idol for a while and want to have the same clothes and toys or to repeat their attitudes. Over time, they realize that they do not have to copy the colleague to have their friendship and stop it. But it is good to be alert when this behavior is exaggerated, asking, for example, why the child wants an object or is doing it. Explain that friendship does not depend on it. If it does not work, seek help from a psychologist. At the other end, the "copied" child can tell his friend, "Be yourself."

Is There Anything Better Than A Long-Standing Friendship?

So that your child does not lose contact with the friends of the first school, you can invest in pajama nights, movie sessions, walks, and activities in which they maintain their coexistence. It's wonderful to keep childhood friends. When there is a story, something special has happened. If a healthy friendship perpetuates itself, it is because it continues to have something to add.

He Said Goodbye

It is evident that friends will leave your child's life for one reason or another. One example is if a friend should move away. This can generate in him an even greater sadness than the simple exchange of school. But how to deal with loss does not change. There are children who suffer less and others, more. This is a frustration that needs to be managed.

You can talk to your child by welcoming him and legitimizing his feelings, without neglecting this pain, at the risk of him becoming even more distressed. At the same time, it is important to encourage him to find resources to face this situation, either by making new friends - by fostering encounters with other children - by maintaining contact with the friend who moved. Through social networks, for example, it is easy to establish video or text conversations among children, even though they live in different countries. They can also be encouraged to send letters, emails, pictures, and drawings to each other.

Beach Friendship

The holidays are fun and pass by fast. Therefore, they are usually so intense for the child. When she makes a good friend on the trip and shares pleasant moments with him, it can be painful to say goodbye. Here, the same tips apply when the friend changes a school or a city. Explain that there are moments of farewell in life, but that it is possible to keep in touch. It may be that the feeling of loss still lasts a few months, but the child has the power to reorganize very quickly.

We all want our children to behave well. In fact, most of us would dare to say that we want our children to be friends with each other. Unfortunately, parents who dream of their children playing together as they grow up usually feel more like judges who never take vacations.

Although we are still trying to figure out how things work with three children, we had our first two children seven years ago. They get on very well. Part of that is personality, and another part of it is because we try to intentionally create an environment where they would grow up and naturally become friends.

Here are some tips I and more importantly, we, as a community, have learned to cultivate friendship between siblings:

1. Give Them Space

Our nine-year-old son needs some time alone. He needs silence and needs rest because of his older brother's role. Even if you do not do this every day, we've talked to him since he became a brother, and whenever he wants, he can spend time alone in his room.

We respect and protect that time, which often means keeping younger siblings away from his room. By being introverted, I understand his need to be alone and in silence to rest. Our two young children do not need time alone, and that's not a problem. But by respecting Will's needs, we're helping them understand that people have different needs. This will help Will to remain patient with his brother and sister, and will also give the two younger ones time to play together. We also never forced them to play together. We respect their literal and figurative space.

2. Do Not Force Them To Share

At least not everything. We think sharing is a lot easier when you do not have to share everything. Let the children have at least some toys or books that are only for each of them. They can share these things when and if they want to. They cannot go into each other's rooms and mess up what is not theirs without permission. Being a child is already too difficult. Having personal properties makes things a little easier. This is also a great way to teach boundaries.

3. Form a Team

No, you do not have to have enough children to form a team literally. But you can promote a teamwork environment within your family. When we do something together, even if it's something small like cleaning the car (okay, that's usually a big task) or something even bigger like finishing a long walk when we all wanted to give up, we celebrated our teamwork. This also applies to the way we talk to them when they are away from us. They know that they must always be united because they are a team.

4. Limit The Time With Friends

We value the friendships they have, but at these ages, most of the time with friends is during class time or at baseball practice. When they play at home, sometimes they are together with a friend, but usually, they play together. And they like it. Because the time of watching TV is limited, their imagination is free to explore while they build memories together.

5. Stop Judging

Unless your children are about to hurt each other, try not to interfere. If we constantly control their quarrels, we will be teaching them that we do not trust them to be able to resolve by themselves.

And no matter what we say, each of them will probably feel like we're taking sides.

Problem-solving is a very valuable skill, but your child will not have a chance to learn if you volunteer to do it for him all the time. And believe me, we know it's tempting, even if it's just to get some quiet time.

6. Invest Quality Time for Each of Your Children

Even though this seems like one more way to build the parent-child relationship, and it really is, it's also a great way to combat sibling rivalry. When the children's love reserve is full, they are much less likely to compete for parental attention. Because they already have it.

Sibling rivalry is normal and cannot be completely eliminated, but I'm not even sure if it should be. Even if listening to your fighting kids drives you crazy, you know they are learning valuable skills that they will use for the rest of their lives. Our first interactions with other people in life are usually with siblings. It's a great way to teach our kids to relate to others, solve problems, and be kind when they do not want to be kind. These are just some of the ways we help our children be friends with each other.

Chapter 7: Discipline

Nowadays, the question of limits and punishments seems to be in everybody's head. Parents are always looking for ways to discipline their children that are fair and effective, so they do not feel guilty for traumatizing the little ones. We quickly learn that our children grow up and that getting punished and other methods of discipline that work on younger children have little or no effect on older children. After all, sending a teenager to sit at a designated time-independent location will not work for its purpose.

As children grow effective punishment requires a whole new approach. An effective measure to discipline older children is to remove the privileges they enjoy. Like, for example, taking a cell phone, iPod, television, or video game. But it is important to be sure that punishment fits the "crime." For example, do not arbitrarily take your phone and give it back when you feel like it. Just as with time, any punishment you put in place should have limits and set rules in order to be effective. Punishment should be proportional to failure, and it is always desirable that they are combined in advance.

A minor infraction should result in the removal of a privilege for a relatively short period of time. Save the most serious punishments for times when your child really does something wrong. In addition, it is always good to explain to the child why you chose such an attitude to punish him, and exactly what you expect from your child in order to have their privileges again.

Lack of discipline hinders learning, professional performance, and even prevents people from reaching their goals in life. Therefore, it is important to learn to be disciplined. As children, we are able to understand routines established by society, and this is good for both group-living and personal fulfillment. Each activity has date, place and time to happen. The task is to be done at home.

The child needs pre-established routines to develop discipline. They need to know clearly what to do, when, how, and what we expect from them in each situation. Many children who seek the cerebral gymnastics course have difficulty learning and have poor results in school. In many cases, it is noted that this is a consequence of a lack of discipline.

To help these children improve their behavior, sometimes parents and schools develop pre-scripted lessons to be given to the child. This eases anxiety and helps a lot. Children pay more attention and carry out activities successfully.

Games Help Develop Discipline

There are examples where schools have developed various kinds of infographics to explain to the child what is expected of him in each activity to be developed. One of the classroom activities that most encourages discipline in the age group of 6 to 10 years is the pedagogical games, which teach the student to obey rules, respect the rights and limits of others and organize the space used for the plays.

Discipline is something that comes from home, but if the child still does not have it, the school needs to give him the necessary stimulus. Here, I would really like to reinforce that discipline contributes incredibly to concentration, reasoning, creativity, memory, self-esteem, and the health of the mind.

How Can Parents Contribute?

Many parents stay at work all day and resent leaving their children at home with no activities to do. There's no television. So the greatest tip of the pedagogue is to create a daily agenda with the tasks that children must do after school.
Write down on a paper the activity and time that the task should be completed. Vary activities each day. You have to be a bit methodical with the child. Leave a clear and objective list with bath time, television, homework, and jokes. Create a

study routine, teach him how to organize room space. Organization is very important.

Another good tip is to set aside time for free activities. The little ones are going to adopt this!

Are days when your little angel looks more like a little devil?

Here are some good practices for educating and disciplining your child which have been gathered from across viewpoints, training and curriculums:

Educating and disciplining children implies, among other things, establishing clear rules and limits. This is not always easy, even more so these days, but if parents adopt positive educational practices early on, it is possible to prevent future difficulties and problems. Cláudia Madeira Pereira, a clinical and health psychologist with a doctorate in clinical psychology, points out some good practices that will make this task easier:

1. Talk To Your Child

Even if you are exhausted after a day at work, take some time out of your day to talk to your child. At dinner or before going to bed, ask him how his day was, using phrases such as "Tell me what you did today," "Tell me about the good things that happened today" or "Did something bad happen?"

If your child is having a bad day, he can resort to several solutions. First, allow him to speak and listen to him without judgment or criticism. If you prefer, look for positive aspects that you can highlight and praise. Also, tell him about "what" and "how" to better deal with similar situations in the future.

2. Pay Attention To Good Behavior

Sometimes children learn that bad behavior is the best way to get parental attention ... This is especially true for children whose parents pay attention to them only when they misbehave, even if that attention is negative, scolding them and rebuking them.

In order for your child to see that the best way to get their attention is through good behavior, praise him / her and / or offer affectionate gestures (giving him kisses and hugs) whenever he does or even tries to do something good, such as helping set the table or doing a message, for example.

3. Promote Your Child's Autonomy And Responsibility

Some tasks, such as dressing in the morning, can be difficult for children. Even though it would be quicker for you to dress your child, you would prefer to encourage their autonomy and responsibility. Help your child by giving short and simple instructions on how to do the tasks.

To do this, use expressions such as "Take off your pajamas," "Now put on your shirt" or "Finally, put on your pants." Finish with a compliment, using phrases like "All right, you did a good job!" Sometimes it will not be enough to tell your child what to do; you may need to show him "what" and "how" to do it.

4. Establish Clear Rules

Be clear with your child about a set of rules. First, explain the rule succinctly and concretely. Second, make sure your child understands the rule and knows what is expected of him. In order for your child to be able to respect the rules more easily, try to give clear and simple directions, empathically and positively.

Phrases like "It's time to go to bed. Let's go to the room now, and then I'll read you a story," usually work. It is common for children to challenge the rules in the early days but stay firm and consistent. Repeat as many times as necessary so that your child realizes that the new rule is to be followed.

5. Set Limits

When you need to correct your child's behavior, try to be patient, and stand firm. Tell your child that a certain behavior must stop, explain the reasons, and inform him of the consequences of not obeying. In that case, preferably use phrases like "If you keep doing, then ...". Immediately and consistently implement the consequences whenever bad behavior occurs.

But do not resort to punishment or physical punishment (such as beating), as they only aggravate children's behavioral problems. Prefer to take a hobby or an object appreciated by your child for some time.

6. Stop The Tantrums

Although it is not easy, try to ignore the tantrums, not paying attention to the child at such times, as long as there is no danger to the child, of course! If possible, step back and pay attention to it only when the tantrums stop, so that your child realizes that they can only get their attention when they stop throwing tantrums. At that point, prepare yourself, because your child will put him to the test.

At first, it is normal for tantrums to get worse. However, by systematically applying this method, the tantrums will eventually disappear.

Remember that what you want with this is that your child learns that tantrums are no longer a good way to get what you want and that the best way to get the attention of parents is to behave well.

To achieve this, you must be aware of your child's good behavior and value these behaviors whenever they occur, for example, by giving a compliment, a kiss, or a hug. If you do, the child will feel more accompanied.

7. Learn to Control Your Negative Feelings

There are times when any mother or father feels the nerves at the edge of the skin. When this happens, there are several ways you can act. First, make sure that your child is in a safe place (such as a crib or room), then withdraw for a moment to calm down. Then try to do something to help him or her. You can, for example, listen to some music or take a few minutes of meditation. When you feel calmer, go back to your child and start again, using conciliatory phrasing in a sweet tone, like "I felt I did not know what to do, but I do know what to do with it now."

8. Have (A Lot Of) Patience

When you raise your child's communication (verbal and non-verbal) empathic and positive, will be contributing to a healthier and happier relationship between both. Educating and disciplining your child will require a great deal of your time and patience. No wonder they say being a mom and dad is tough, but at the end of the day, it will be well worth it because it is the most rewarding job you can have.

Chapter 8: Connecting

The day to day work is always very hectic. Parents do not stop for a second. I think that everyone who has a child lives the same tiresome routine and always looks for the best way to connect with their child, although this is not always easy. Take care of children, clean the house, organize tasks, and I know that many mothers and fathers find themselves alone in these tasks. They are really like an octopus because they have to deal with a thousand and a few things in a single moment.

With all this upheaval, we can put aside the connection with our children, letting stress overwhelm us. It's easier to leave our kids a little time, maybe two, in front of the TV. Phew, this time gives us a lot of things: sweeping, bathing, tidying up, storing clothes ... The problem is when it becomes a routine, and little by little, it seems easier for us to silence our children by giving them a thousand and one toy so that we have a desired moment of peace.

What we do not tell ourselves is that this moment of peace can cost us dearly. In the end, the disconnection with our children will make us parents ruder, that to get the son to do what he wants, he should scream, curse, threaten, and even beat.

Following some advice can help us to establish an effective connection with our children on a daily basis:

- No cell phone when you are with the child.
- Turn off the television
- Make at least one activity together a day.
- Ask how your day was, listen to it calmly.
- Play
- Observe their behavior.
- Set priorities
- Exclusive time when you are with the child
- Tell him how you feel. Ask him how he feels
- Read stories together

Remember: THE BIGGEST PRESENT YOU CAN give is the best way for you to connect with your child.

Not to complicate things, but if there are simple and effective ways to connect with your child, why not use them? How about opening up space for something like Positive Discipline?

Now, touching upon the topic of positive discipline, we learn to focus on empowering our children so they can become able in solving their problems on their own. We also recognize that physical and psychological punishment are not resources that foster children who are autonomous, responsible, and independent.

I have noticed the frustration of some mothers when they come across a public place with their children and ask themselves: "Am I the only one experiencing these tantrums and moments of desperation? "I see such" nice "children! At this moment, the best thing to do is to be empathetic and very careful in attacking you and your children. You should prefer keeping the connection with children than thinking only of pure discipline. When we keep our attention focused on them, it helps to improve the relationship and achieve success in the strategies we employ.

There is no way we can connect with children without devoting quality time to them. It is not enough for five minutes at breakfast or five minutes before bed. Being wholehearted with children requires us to be willing and "some" time of exclusivity - parents and children - mother and child or other similar combination by combination stress: connection, time, love, dedication, and clarity of family attitudes and agreements.

We are always overwhelmed with everyday tasks. We cannot let life pass like a steamroller over us. How many times have you looked throughout the day for your child and really felt connected to him? Want a better connection than a bear hug, an eye on the eye, and a surprise kiss? Children are not our possessions - they belong to themselves. So we need to hear what's on their minds. What they dream, what they expect from us as parents and their fears. Have you listened to your child carefully?

Think in terms of quality rather than quantity. I'm not referring to being stuck or in the presence of the child 24 hours a day. On the other hand, being at home and not having time for a valued connection is not functional. Being there is simply very different from being connected. If you are doubtful if the time you are dedicating to your child is of quality, ask yourself the following questions: "Have had moments throughout the day where I am really body and soul with my child?" "Have I hugged and told my child that I loved him often enough?"

We are upset or disappointed when our children exhibit inappropriate behavior. We cannot forget that children are immature, and as such, still cannot deal with emotions. Anger, frustration, or sadness may trigger the red button. So we need to remind ourselves that we are the relievers and the blueprint for our children, and most of the time we have to play the 'middle field.' The next time your child goes off the hook or behaves inappropriately, avoid any outbursts of violence and seek more effective solutions. Violent shouts do not educate, but frighten, humiliate, and reduce the child's connection with his caretaker.

Access your power of compassion! We are less tolerant of children than of most adults we live with. Children are still in the process of developing and learning - they need compassion much more than our criticism. The way we respond or react to a particular behavior of our child may mark him for the rest of his life.

Avoid excluding and promoting the connection. When your child does not seem to listen to you or even be aggressive towards another child, it is the moment that he or she needs you most. We have a tendency to reprimand and punish. Avoid doing this - show acceptance and at the right time, talk about what happened. Otherwise, the message you will be passing on to your child is that you only validate it when he is "nice." Remember, there are no perfect parents or perfect kids. We are human, and mistakes are good ways of learning.

Try to see your children as timely teachers. Children are able to awaken the best and the worst in us. In the worst moments, where we feel a lot of anger, our tendency is to go to the attack and punish in several ways: beat, scream, or other forms of punishment. However, instead of pressing children to be our ideals, we can adjust our anxiety or expectations and learn to direct our attention to our own feelings and how to deal with them in the best possible way. We are parents with a strong desire to be right. So we can use our experience as lessons. We can learn to see the world through a childish gaze. In this way, we will learn to be less critical, pessimistic, and punitive.

Be more curious. We tend, as adults, to think we know all the time. Our son will tell us a story and we anticipate counting the end (at least in thought). What we do not know is the size that this story has for our children. Children feel the need to be seen through our curious and loving gaze. So ask more about the characters in the story, get interested in the plot, laugh, be amazed, vibrate, and fantasize along with your child. Just be curious.

What to do for dinner? Who's going to pick up the kids at school today? And if it gets cold, are they well wrapped? There are so many decisions that parents have to take every moment that they often forget to take breaks to enjoy the company of the little ones. It so happens that, in parallel with caring, these moments are also responsible for creating strong and lasting bonds - which is fundamental to your child's cognitive and emotional development early on.

"Children who have strong ties to their parents have greater learning capacity and are better related to each other," says pediatrician Cid Pinheiro, of São Luiz Morumbi Hospital (SP). A survey published this year in Finland proves this. By accompanying 700 families over seven years (from the baby's birth until he entered school), scientists were able to observe that in those children and parents who had healthy relationships, children were more likely to learn to regulate their own emotions.

Another important point is that in these moments of complicity, you get to know much more about your child, their likes, desires, and what he thinks about the world around him. You will be surprised and proud. This exchange is one of many that strengthens the bond with your child. Here are 11 tips to put into practice!

1. Create Family Traditions

Children, especially younger ones, feel safer in well-defined routines. Use this to your advantage, including connecting times with your child throughout the day's activities. For example, sing a song at bath time, serve breakfast in the form of smiling faces (with bread, pancakes, fruit) and even pause together to meditate and relax.

2. Enroll In A Course With The Child

Music, arts or swimming lessons can be a lot more fun with the children on the side, so much so that there are nowadays several establishments that offer courses aimed at children and parents. Prepare to be delighted to witness each new achievement of your child, such as mastering a new step or increasing your breath to stay underwater and see you happy to be able to share it first-hand with you. The partnership in these moments of discovery and learning will make them closer.

3. Take A Different Walk

Who does not remember a sunny morning at the beach or a lazy afternoon fishing with the whole family? Many memories are lost in adulthood, but special moments surrounded by people we love always remain. Even though the effective memories of this phase are not accessible to consciousness, they are still present. Use creativity when deciding the program! It does not have to be anything elaborate, as long as it fades from the routine. A day at the amusement park, a visit to the museum, a picnic in the square ...

4. Read To (And With) Your Child

The tip is basic, but it counts a lot! It is worth, first of all, to create a special climate for the time of reading, whether it is a corner with cushions on the floor or a half-light. Try to interpret the story by giving a different voice to each character to stimulate the imagination. For example: if the character is more thoughtful, speak slowly, and tone down. If he is tense, use a firm voice. And have your child read to you later or make up some story. Besides being a delight to hold while reading, the books are an invitation to the curious questions of the small and almost inexhaustible subject for future conversations.

5. Build a Camp in the Room

Kids love an adventure, and you do not even have to leave the house to fulfill that desire. Put pillows and cushions on the floor and build an improvised tent with the sheets. It's time to disconnect all the electronics and act like you're in a real camp. Connect a flashlight in the dark, tell stories, and enjoy sleeping together. They will not forget that night so soon!

6. Stipulate The Day Of "Today You Can!"

The routine with children is full of rules and schedules, as it has to be. But a little flexibility does well, as well! Did he ask for popcorn on the way out of school? A snack alone will not ruin the whole week's meals. Think about it. These situations teach your child that it is important to be malleable in life and yet will create good memories for you!

7. Play Together

This is also easy, a delight, and one of the activities kids love most about their parents. Joking with paint, building blocks or taking that lying afternoon tea make interaction easier. Forget the mess for a few hours and let the more spontaneous and creative side of your child flow. After all, experimenting is essential for child development, and he will know that you made sure to create that kind of opportunity!

8. Let Him Help At Home

As long as activities are safe, there are only benefits in letting your child participate in household chores. Give him a piece of cloth and see how he enjoys dusting furniture or toys. Another idea is to get help to spread the sheets on the bed, store clothes in the drawers, dry plastic jars. In addition to improving motor coordination, these activities enable the child to develop a sense of responsibility and cooperation, to feel important and even more part of the family.

9. Pay Attention To The Subtleties

Learning to recognize the signs your child gives through gestures and body expressions, especially when he does not yet master speech, is a skill that strengthens the relationship. To become a master in this art, there is only one way: to pay attention. Something that seems obvious, but that can be left in a rush. So, soon you will begin to understand that that sly cry is synonymous with tiredness, what are the foods he likes best and when it is time to take a nap. And he will feel secure knowing that you understand his desires.

10. Take Photos, Make Videos...

Take a few minutes (OK, you can last for hours, get ready!) to see your child's photo albums and yours. He will love to see himself when he was little, to know what he did next to his parents, what he already said, he did ... And show his memories too. Then enjoy making funny selfies and videos (with those filters that kids love) and save them for new memories opportunities like that in the future.

11. Fill Him With Kisses And Hugs

Ah ... the best part, no? Showing affection physically is one of the most natural ways to maintain a close relationship - not to mention that touch stimulates nerve endings in the skin that promote well-being. Since you die of wanting to grab your child every time you see those cheeks even, do not hold back! Now, if he does not like hugging and kissing, that's okay. Find other ways to connect by touch, such as combing hair, moisturizer, walking hand in hand, doing a delicious massage on his feet ... And do not forget: being together is all that really matters.

Chapter 9: Toddlers: Communicating

The desire for independence: In order to become a responsible adult, your child must, as it were, move slowly from the passenger seat to the driver's seat and learn to drive the tortuous paths of life.

For children, everything is black or white For example, for a child, the concept of justice is simple: 'Mama broke a cookie and gave half to me, half to my brother.' In this case, justice comes down to a mathematical formula. Abstract thinking helps your child draw his or her own conclusions about complex issues. But this has a downside: his conclusions may be contrary to yours.

What You Can Do

Have relaxed conversations. Enjoy the moments when your child is more comfortable to talk. Be brief. You do not need to give a long sermon to every problem. Say what needs to be said and stop there. This may take effect later. When your child is alone, he will be able to think better about what you said. Give him a chance to do it.

Listen and be flexible. To get a full picture of the problem, listen carefully - without interrupting. When you say something, be reasonable. If you stick to the rules too much, your child will be tempted to look for loopholes. That's where the children begin to lead a double life. They tell parents what parents want to hear, but they do what they like when they are away from them.

Whenever possible, give guidance instead of orders. Your child's ability to think abstractly is like a muscle that needs to be exercised. So when he has to make a decision, do not do the "exercise" for him. When discussing the problem, let it suggest some solutions. Then say something like, "Now that you have given some options think of them for a day or two. Then we can talk about which one you prefer and why".

Starting from the point that parents are the best friends of children and they just want to see their happiness and satisfaction, why not be the best medium of information for them? And be able to help them?

There are many factors that cause a lack of intimacy between parents and their children, making it difficult for the family to communicate:

- Lack of meetings during meals
- Parents work late and hardly see their children
- At weekends, kids prefer television, video games or the internet than sit down for a family conversation

- When they are with their parents, the children do not expose their problems because they feel ashamed, the contact is so little that sometimes it is better to talk with a friend in the school with whom they live every day and for a certain time, than to talk with the father and mother who only finds the night and so little.

It's hard to really communicate with someone you do not know well. Do you know your child? Children need to feel that adults trust them. Many, given the opportunity, will be worthy of the trust deposited in them. And it is very good for parents to be able to speak openly and honestly about their own youth, as they did then. It shows off a high degree of confidence. Young people who can communicate with their parents are much happier and more confident. Sincere communication is the number one priority for young people. Efficient communication is based on:

- Having mutual trust.
- Show frankness and honesty.
- Be able to forgive and go forward.
- Respect privacy.
- Avoid joking and scorn.
- Maintain good humor and willingness to make real compliments
- Leave there the usual problems.
- Be able to listen and then talk.

- Move away and choose a better time when you are angry.
- Do not make accusations.

Showing interest in the children's lives is proving that parents care about them. Do you know the answers to these questions?

What is the name of your child's best friends? Have you been introduced to them yet? Do you know where they live? What kind of book, movie, and sport does your child enjoy? What is his team? What kind of music does he like? Do you know if you have any special subject, any area or hobby your child is interested in? If he practices a sport, do you know what position he plays on the team? When was the last time you went to see him play?

It is extremely important to fraternal friendship. Children need their parents more than ever, the world each day is complicated in a frightening way, several problems afflict young people, and that is why the family needs to see the lack of communication and a more intimate relationship. All major modern things, such as TV, the Internet, and advertising, contributed to the family changing their habits, greatly facilitating the lives of individuals. The truth is that there is a lack of interest of the parents in the universe of the children and vice-versa, but this has a solution, it is enough to want and to be involved.

Children with more access to language can hear up to 30 million more words by age 4 than children in unfavorable situations. How does access to language affect the development and learning of infants and toddlers? US pediatric surgeon Dana Suskind went on to investigate this issue by operating hearing-impaired babies.

She realized that among babies who received cochlear implants (deaf implants), those who best developed the ability to communicate were those who lived in homes where there were more dialogue, more interaction and more variety of vocabulary.

Their perceptions were reinforced by a 1995 study that had identified that children with less access to language (many of whom were in poverty) were able to hear 30 million fewer words accumulated up to four years of age compared to others in poorer situations favorable - and the latter were more prepared upon entering school, had richer vocabulary, more fluency in reading, and, consequently, achieved higher grades.

Since a large part of the brain growth is completed at the age of four, "children who dropped out front (in terms of language) were still ahead, those who started with lags were left behind," the study said. 'Despacito' does not leave your head? Science explains the success of the music-gum 'Children are living like rats': the plight of Mosul survivors after the expulsion of the Islamic State. To reduce these language differences in children from needy families, Suskind created in Chicago, USA , the Thirty Million Words Initiative, a program that, since motherhood and in pediatric visits, teaches parents about the importance of talking and interacting with babies from their first day of life, to stimulate the construction of new neural connections in the small brain that forms.

One of the specialist's suggestions is to tune into what your child is doing and take advantage of this to talk. The program has now been expanded to other areas of the United States, and Suskind - who is also a professor at the University of Chicago - wrote a book based on the experience: Thirty Million Words - Building a Child's Brain (Thirty Million Words - Building the Free Child Brain).

In an interview with BBC Brazil, she teaches ideas on how to use the language productively to stimulate the child's brain, which I also agree with strongly.

1. To Have Your Child As A 'Conversation Partner'

One of the first lessons of the Thirty Million Words is something intuitive for parents: to react to the sounds, looks, and gestures of the baby from birth, in a natural and integrated way to everyday life.

"If you are changing his diaper or taking a bus, explain this to the baby. It is an opportunity to enrich his vocabulary and show the relationship between a particular sound and the act to which it belongs."

Suskind cites research that shows that going beyond basic conversation - "come here," "put on your shoes," "eat your food," is a crucial point in developing children's language.

This is what she calls "extra talk," that is, dialogue with the child and the environment around her and stimulate the conversations: "what a big tree!"; "Who is the boy with the dirty diaper?"; "What is the taste of this food?"; "What do you think happened to the character in that book?"

The quantity of words is only part of the equation. The quality of the conversation is important - the richness of the vocabulary, the comings and goings of the conversation, the way you speak.

It is important to see your baby as a partner in conversations from the very first day of life.

2. Helping To Develop Mathematical Skills

Parents can help develop children's spatial sense and mathematical skills simply by talking about it.

If you use mathematical and spatial concepts - for example, counting your toes and hands, comparing the size of a triangle, using words that refer to the different shapes of objects - it will help prepare children to learn math.

A University of Chicago study asked four-year-olds to pick up punch cards drawn on them to correspond to a number (for example: when you hear the number five, pick up the card with five points drawn). And he discovered that children who had been exposed to more mathematical vocabulary and spatial notions were able to make more correct correspondences.

Moreover, Suskind argues, it is precisely in "mathematical conversations" that an important gender disparity occurs. A study of middle and upper-middle-class mothers showed that daughters as young as two heard half the mathematical conversations of their children. This may alienate girls from fields that may interest them ... Girls who hear that math is 'not their forte' often do not do well in math."

3. Speak Positively, But Praise The Effort More Than The Child

According to Suskind, children in needy families can hear more than double negative comments - "you're spoiled"; "you're wrong" - for an hour than children in families in a better socioeconomic situation.

They also hear less praise. And since these children tend to listen to fewer words in general, these negative expressions end up having a greater weight in their cognitive development. What will it be like repeatedly to hear that you never do anything right? It's a difficult child environment to overcome. The difference between prohibition words ('do not do it,' 'stop') and encouragement ('very well') is great. It causes stress in the brain to hear them repeatedly. It is important to try to change orders for a more productive conversation.

But if negative and prohibitive language can be a barrier to development and learning, is the answer always to praise - and constantly say that your child is incredible and intelligent?

There has been researching, showing that this kind of praise can, rather than empower future adults, only leave them passive and dependent on the opinion of others. What we are looking for is not the eyes facing themselves, happy with self-satisfaction, but children who see a task and, no matter how challenging it may be, can almost immediately think how it can be fulfilled. It's what parents want: adults stable, constructive, motivated.

The way to do this, according to the studies analyzed by Suskind, is to recognize and praise not only the child, but the effort and commitment of it in their daily activities, the use of other words, instead of just saying "you're too smart" to a girl who turned a difficult puzzle, go further: "I saw you struggled to finish and succeeded. Very well! "

Suskind suggests looking for day-to-day moments when the child has stood out. The child is still learning what it is to behave well. Pointing these moments to her reinforces the idea of what that means.

4. Stimulate Autonomy Rather Than Just Obedience

Suskind quotes two sentences that can be said to a child in the same context:

"Now store your toys."

"What should we do with toys after we've finished playing?"

"The first sentence is an order that must be fulfilled without questioned. The second sentence, however, supports the autonomy of the child. One-year-old babies whose mothers are quietly suggesting, rather than ordering, behavioral rules have gained executive function and self-regulation by the age of four "- which are our ability to stay focused on a problem instead of react explosively and violently. Parents who use the pressure and the authority to restrict the child's behavior can get obedience in the short term, but in the long, are creating conditions for low self-regulation (the child).

The least efficient method of constructing brain connections because it is the most efficient method of constructing brain connections require no or little language response. It may be more efficient, instead of just saying" put on your shoes, "explaining what is behind the request and the relationship between cause and effect of things:" It's time to go to school. glue, so it's good to put your shoes on to keep your feet dry and warm. Please go get them."

5. Tune In To The Child - And Indulge In The" Baby Voice"

Suskind recommends paying attention to what is arousing the child's interest - a joke, an object - and turn it around on the topic of conversation. Another example: The father or mother, with the best of intentions, sits on the floor next to the child with a children's book in their hands. But the child does not pay attention and continues to play with his toy, snobbery the adult. The parent gives direct and short orders like "sit," "stay quiet," and "do not do it." Now, these are the least efficient method of building brain connections because they require little or no language response.

How about instead of imposing the reading of the book, entering into the child's play and talking about it? Parents learn to become aware of what their children are doing and become part of it, helping to develop practiced ability the play and, through verbal interaction, the child's brain. Tuning in also involves, according to her, to take every opportunity to read and sing with the child - or even speak with that infantile voice that many of us use with babies.

"That sung voice is a rich nutrient for the baby's brain because it helps him understand the sounds of words," explains Suskind. Here's one more warning: An easy way to lose that harmony with children and infants is to be distracted by the cell phone during the game. Smartphones are taking the place of personal interaction with infants and children. It is only when the child is the primary focus of parents that attention is needed for optimal brain development.

Chapter 10: Family Routines

How Can Routine Help Your Child?

We know that in practice, it is not easy to establish a routine in the lives of children, especially with the rush of everyday life, irregular hours, and lack of time. However, it is very important that the family adopt some habits and rules in the daily life of the little ones. A routine for children, from an early age, helps them to grow more confident and independent. Knowing what will happen during the day, and repeating these events creates a healthy environment, making the children feel comfortable and safe.

Little ones like to know what will happen during their day. Knowing that, after a nap, is the snack or that, before bed, is the story, provides a sense of security. This makes the little ones feel less anxious. Over time, the routine can even cause your baby to develop certain mania, such as sleeping with the same blanket or just eating certain foods. It is the way they have to feel in control, in this world still so foreign to them.

Benefits for Dads and Moms

For parents, pre-established routines also bring many benefits. First, because they feel more secure, the little ones tend to accept the farewell moments better. For example, the time to leave the playground or say goodbye when parents go to work does not become so difficult because they understand that they will return. Thus, from an early age, the little ones will understand and assimilate the schedules and rules of everyday life. When they grow up, they become children and adolescents with a greater sense of organization and responsibility, being able to establish study and bonding schedules, such as helping the family in household activities. In addition, routines also help organize the life of parents. Having established schedules for meals, naps, showers, and games, makes the whole family organize better and have more time to enjoy the moments together.

Know How To Be Flexible

It is important to remember that the excess is never good and therefore not worth turning the house into a barracks! You have to know the time to be flexible so that the routine does not become something negative. On weekends, for example, you are allowed to sleep a few more hours or have lunch later. The important thing is to set schedules and create healthy habits that make the environment more organized and comfortable for everyone!

Bedtime

Bedtime is the first routine idea of the little ones, and they need to know the difference between day and night. Naps during the day should always be in a clear environment, without disturbing noises or changing the routine of the house.

For night sleep parents need to perform "sleep hygiene" as a ritual. It can be a relaxing bath, followed by a story. The room should be dimly lit and free of noise.

Time To Feed

It is healthy to have family meals, all seated at the table and tasting varied foods. Take the opportunity to talk and realize that your little one is growing. You can also enjoy setting up a new menu for the following week.

Establish Schedules

It is important that children have schedules to wake up, carry out activities, play, and sleep. Following the schedule makes the child get used to it and establishes a routine. You can assemble for your little one a timesheet with drawings, showing what will be the order of your day, this will bring more security to him.

Organized Spaces

Having an organized environment will help the little ones. For this to happen, it is very important that they know that:

- After playing, they should store their toys
- Used clothes should be placed in the basket

From an early age, the little ones can and should help with the housework, after all, they are also part of the house!

What Is The Importance Of Routine For The Child?

Routine exerts a fundamental influence on child development. Among other factors, it teaches the child to live with family and even community reality (neighborhood, school, etc.), in addition to contributing to the strengthening of autonomy. But only 15% of the population considers it important that the child up to 3 years of age have a routine (food, bath, hours to watch television, etc.).

What Exactly Is Routine?

Value the role of routine in early childhood, always respecting diversity. Each family has its own way of working. In communication, reinforce that children should have sleep, food, hygiene, and playtime and that this is good for their development.

What Are The Benefits Of Routine For The Child?

The establishment of the routine is very important for the child and for his adult life. The adult you will be, depends on your experience as a child. Childhood is when you establish a strong sense of self and routine reinforces a positive self-image. In this sense, the benefits of the routine can be summarized as: In order for the child to feel safe, he has to acquire positive and healthy habits from the beginning. Children do not know the order of things when they are born, and so it is adults who must teach them to organize their lives through schedules associated with routines, that is, through activities they must do every day in the same way.

The repetition of rituals helps the child to assimilate an inner scheme that makes the world a predictable and therefore safe place.

Food, sleep, and hygiene are the first habits that children have to learn. The daily routine is for children what the walls are for the home; it gives them limits and dimensions of life. The routine gives a sense of security. The established routine gives a sense of order from which freedom is born.

143

What Do Habits And Routines For Children Mean?

The routine is a personal custom established by your coexistence and does not allow modification, that is, it is inflexible, safeguarded some very specific situations that are beyond our control, such as unforeseen events. The habit is a stable mechanism that creates skills and can be used in a variety of situations, such as putting on seat belts. Habits are customs, attitudes, behaviors, or behaviors that imply learning. The well-used and used habit allows us to face everyday events.

Habits and routines contribute to constancy and regularity, important mechanisms, and therefore are fundamental for both family and school life.

What Are The Consequences Of Lack Of Routine For The Child?

Not having a basic routine brings behavioral problems that can be considered inconvenient by an inexperienced professional; in school, the child may present difficulties that are often also perceived as Learning Disorders. In addition, the child becomes disorganized, giving more work than usual. The construction of the personality can also be affected since the routine has limits and rules necessary and fundamental for the construction of the character of the person. Children crave control, just as adults do. Without a routine, they may feel that they have none, and this can result in anxiety and tantrums.

How Can We Establish A Healthy Routine For Children?

First of all, be aware of what each child can do at the age they are. Give autonomy forever. Do not raise your children as if they were princes or princesses. They need to learn early on that they are ordinary people just like any other. Time to sleep, wake up, play.

Create habits and rules: brush your teeth after meals, do the chores first, and play later.

Teach them to organize their own objects and toys.

Always speak the truth so that the child does not learn to lie at home.

At mealtimes and on homework, the TV, tablet, and mobile phone should be out of the reach of the child so as not to compete with what needs to be done.

Teach your children that you, parents, are the people of authority at home! Children do not tell their parents what to do but can instead share their opinions on a subject. Be in charge, but don't forget to be flexible and remember that you are growing tiny adults. You must be the people of affective and authoritative reference to your children. Do not delegate to others the education and rearing of your children. The real presence of the parents is fundamental to the development of the child. Stay tuned to the way they talk, how they dress, how they behave. Your children observe your ways of being and adopt your habits as their own. Sometimes the behavioral problem that the child presents originates from the home itself.

Follow the evolution of your children in school, and in the face of difficulties, seek help as soon as possible. Take care of your children's self-esteem! Do not call them by nicknames and/or negative words. This affects the self-esteem and emotional growth of your children. Set small tasks so that the children also contribute to the proper functioning of the house.

And remember, a well-educated child from an early age will be a responsible and happy adult in the future!

Making Family – Make Children Confident!

What is breakfast like at your house? So much rush that your son can only finish the sandwich inside the car? And at dinner is everyone so tired that all you can do is throw yourself on the couch and eat some pasta? Okay, we know routine is crazy now, but - maybe - it's time to rethink some habits.

A survey of 34,000 children and adolescents from the Literacy Trust, an English institution dedicated to literacy and reading encouragement, concluded that talking during meals helps raise more confident children. To reach this result, the children responded as it was the time of the meals in their homes and some questions that indirectly evaluated their social and communicative abilities.

The survey found that 87 percent of the children sat with their families during the meal, but one in four did not talk to their parents or siblings. Among those who always ate with their parents and talked during meals, 75% said they feel comfortable to participate in classroom discussions. Among those who did not talk, that number dropped to 57%. When asked how they felt about talking in front of friends in the class, in the first group, 62% said they felt good compared to 47% in the second. Through these parameters, those in charge of the research concluded that talking during meals is a great tool for children and parents.

Research shows the importance of family communication. A table is a place that favors this union because people need to be seated if they look in the eye, and the dialogue happens. But these exchanges should not happen only in those moments.

For families living in large urban centers, it is difficult to demand that they make the three meals together. The tip is to try to reserve at least one of them to sit down and eat calmly. If a parent has no time to get home, try to organize the routine in the morning for family coffee. If the nights are quieter, eat together for dinner. The most important thing is that the meal is well-made, and you have time to talk. Knowing how the day was, what's new at school, if he's enjoying swimming lessons, if he's spoken to his grandmother. The main thing is interaction and that parents show interest in their children's lives.

If your family's routine is too rushed or if your children are still small and make meals much earlier than the rest of the house, do not despair. Although the table is a strong symbol of family unity, you can reinvent the moments of coexistence. Keeping this dialogue while you are stuck in traffic with the kids in the car, telling bedtime stories and enjoying every weekend minute are viable alternatives for busy families.

Another important tip: do not let the technology stay between you. At mealtime, turn off the television. Check emails on your smartphone? Forget. Leave to use these accessories when alone.

What Does The Family Meal Do For You?

According to nutritionist Marisa Resende Coutinho, from São Camilo Hospital (SP), family meals are fundamental for the formation of food habits. The younger children are still learning to eat. We need to put food on the table, make them taste, and see what they're eating.

In addition, watching what parents are eating stimulates the child's curiosity. Parents are a great example in relation to food. It's no good if you want your child to eat carrots if he's never seen you do it. The same goes for foods that you do not want to present to your child: if the idea is to delay soda intake, for example, avoid taking that tin in front of the children - they are sure to ask you to try it!

From 6 months on, it's time to introduce solid foods into your child's diet. At about 10 months, your child is already able to sit, so you can stay in the high chair by the table. If it is already adapted to the solids, there is no problem in offering the same food as the parents, provided it is prepared with a little seasoning. Another difference is that the food should cook a bit more to become softer and facilitate the ingestion.

Chapter 11: Rules And Consequences

Everything that is little has grace, but when the little one realizes that he has his own wills, grace can turn into disgrace! We speak, of course, of the phases of tantrums, spoiled, and uncontrollable children who do not give us rest. Like any human being, kids also need basic rules to be able to explore and avenge in their little world ... without leaving their parents on the verge of a fit of nerves.

The Importance of Rules and Limits

The American pediatrician Berry Brazelton says that "for children to grow well, they need only love and limits" - love is fundamental to growing with confidence and self-esteem; limits are crucial for the child to learn self-control so that he can live in a family and in society. That is, with respect to the rules of behavior at home (and out of it!) Is really "small that twists the cucumber." Education starts at home, and you do not have to feel guilty for being too strict - children become balanced adults because they lived by rules and limits, not the other way around.

Few And Good

Child behavior studies show that children respond very well to rules, provided they are simple and limited in quantity. Once the child is old enough to see what is right and wrong, make the rules that are appropriate to their age, clearly and one at a time, so as not to confuse them. It is better to memorize fewer than none. Without losing authority or making many concessions, try to maintain some flexibility: for example, when explaining to the child this or that situation, give them three possible scenarios, asking them to give their opinion as to which way to go. In addition to engaging and fostering their independence, it makes limit enforcement less rigid and less "heavy," with "negotiation" being the easiest way for kids to learn to respect the rules. Of course, establishing and imposing limits on your little angels will sometimes cost you (it's a normal feeling), it will not be easy, and it will take time. But patience, love, and joint learning will give precious help.

How To Set Rules

When you want to implement a rule, talk to your child calmly, explaining what you want as clearly as possible, asking you several times if you have questions. Explain to him the consequences of non-compliance with the rules. The "punishments" should be very clear and executable, that is, do not say that you will deprive you of watching television for a week if you know that you will never have the courage to do so. Give the child some freedom in complying with the rules, that is, if he knows that at 9:00 pm he has clean up the toys, brush his teeth and get to bed, let him choose what he wants to do first. Rules can also be fun!

I Was Wrong!

If the child "threatens" does not comply with one of the rules, give him a 5-minute warning, speaking calmly but seriously and remind him of the consequences. After checking that the rule has not been fulfilled or has been partially fulfilled, ask why the child did not do it, explain how you do it (in case you had any difficulty) or help him finish the task, saying that for the next it will be able to do it alone. The easiest way for a child to try to get out of complying with their rules is to make a tantrum. However, adults should never give in to children's tantrums. If you get to the point where punishment is necessary, do not hesitate to stick to it, that is, do not change your mind, do not change the "promised" punishment - otherwise you may get the idea that the consequences are not real and does or does not enforce the rules.

You Did Well!

Do not focus too much on bad behavior and try to give equal attention to good behavior. When children put their books away or wash their hands without anyone telling you anything, praise and pamper them - there is nothing that children enjoy more than being the target of parental attention (for a good reason!), so it is natural that they continue to behave well, just to continue to draw their attention. When the child behaves and asks for something calmly and politely, consider making him feel comfortable.

Some of the best rules you can establish for children to behave well:

Establishing rules for children is fundamental to early childhood education because it is through them that it is possible to teach limits and develop the capacity to live in society. However, it is not enough just to determine what your child can and cannot do: you need to explain why these standards exist and are so important.

Many parents believe that children cannot assimilate this kind of information, but that is a mistake. Despite their young age, children are able to absorb and understand a lot of information. Of course, they do not have the same degree of understanding as adults, but they can already understand some important aspects of rules and norms.

Parents need not only cherish the physical and mental health of their children but also provide a quality education so that they can live in society, respecting the limits of the child and understanding how the mechanisms work. To help you make your child behave, we have mentioned some rules for children that all parents must put into practice.

Always greet and say goodbye when in any setting

No matter if the child is in the home, at school, or anywhere else, she needs to say hello and say goodbye to the people who are present in the environment in which he finds himself. That's a way for him always to tell us when he's here or when he's leaving. More than that: this is a basic etiquette standard for any occasion.

Tidying Up Everything He Has Disrupted, Or Parents Ask For

This is perhaps one of the rules for older children to teach the child. Your child needs to be aware that everything he or she takes off must be replaced immediately after use. This is true for toys, books, clothes, etc. But it's not just what the child has messed with. He needs to be aware that the family environment is a space of shared coexistence, so everyone needs to help.

Laying the table, taking things to the sink, helping folding clothes, are little organizing activities that will make all the difference in her future.

Always Use "Please" When You Ask For Something

This word, "please," may seem like just details, but it makes all the difference in kindergarten. With it, the child understands that it is necessary to ask for things with education, to be attended to (if possible), and not just imposing their will.

This is one of the rules for children that needs to be constantly demonstrated by parents. If the child sees the mother or father demanding things without asking please, of course, she will imitate them. So it's up to the parents to set the example accordingly.

Apologizing

Knowing how to make a mistake is another fundamental item for early childhood education, as this will directly interfere with the child's personality in the future. A child who does not assume that he has done the wrong thing will become an inconsequential adult, who will have no remorse for wrongdoings, even if they harm others.

A good way to encourage and teach your child to apologize is to decrease your punishment. If he makes a mistake and promises that he will no longer commit (or will only try to avoid) the punishment should be less. But he needs attention so that he does not end up apologizing just for not being punished.

No Swearing

This is also one of the rules for children that many parents have difficulty teaching to children. This is often because they themselves cannot control vocabulary around children, or because they end up being exposed to such words in other settings, such as at school or at family events, for example.

In order for children to not speak profanity, the first step is for parents to cut off this kind of language from day to day. Remember: you are the mirror of your child. If this type of verbiage is used in other settings such as a family party, get close to relatives and explain that you do not want them to use these words so that the child is not influenced.

Not Playing With Food Or Grumbling At The Table

This is a common household problem. The child seems just to want to play, or if he does not like something, he grumbles how much he hates a certain type of food. In those hours, it takes patience. Sit down with your child and explain why he should be polite to the table, not complaining about the food. If he does not like something, like vegetables (which is very common), explain how important they are to his health, to growing. Do all this without forgetting, of course, to lead by example, behaving well at the table and having a healthy diet.

Do Not Waste

Sustainability is also a subject that must be present when it comes to teaching rules for children. They need to learn that every little thing, whether it's a lighted light or a dripping faucet, makes all the difference for the protection of the environment.

Teach the child never to waste things. When leaving an environment, always turn off the light, close the taps well, do not put on the dish what he will not be able to eat, among other things. In this way, it will create environmental awareness from an early age.

Always Pay Attention When Someone Is Talking To You And Talk Politely

The last of the rules for children fundamental to early childhood education is that the child is always educated. This should be present, whether in the way of talking to other adults or children or listening to someone talking to them. This teaching will interfere with her whole life. For the child to learn this, obviously parents need to set an example. If the child wants to tell you something, do not ignore it or pretend to listen. Give the attention he needs. The same goes for talking to him: be polite and keep the tone appropriate for the conversation.

What Mistakes To Avoid So Rules For Children Work

Many parents complain that they try to teach rules for children, but it seems that they do not change anything in the way they are. Probably this is because you, as a parent, are committing one of the following errors:

- Do not impose limits of truth, just speak the rules to children out of mouth
- Teach one thing, but do another
- Do not remember every day how important these standards are
- Just introduce the rules for children without explaining why they exist.

Those are just a few mistakes. By avoiding them, you will find it much easier to educate your child. It is these vices that many adults have that end up harming the child's learning, causing it to repeat the same bad habits of the parents. When teaching rules for children, always keep in mind that this is a continuous and joint work. This means that it needs to happen on a daily basis and that parents also need to show that they are following the same standards so that the child understands that it is valid for all.

Educating children is a complicated task. It requires creativity, authority, persistence, determination ... As each child acts in a way, some parents are more likely to impose limits than others. But it's obvious that they all need to set rules for the little ones to respect. Punishment? Spanking? Conversation?

Each one has his way of acting, which can please others or not. But there are some basic tips that all parents (and grandparents, uncles ...) can follow and that help in the education of a child. However, this is not a cake recipe. Each family needs to fit their reality and the reality of their child. It does not cost a try.

1 - Limit For The Children, Not For The Parents

You establish a rule and impose it for your child. However, it requires that you also follow it. This is very common in the education process, but it cannot always be applied. The limits are for the children, not for the parents. It is the children who are being educated, not their parents. It's always good to keep that in mind.

It is obvious that parents need to be the example; this is very important for the fixation of learning. But it is essential to know that this part of each adult is not an obligation, nor is it allowed for the little ones to dictate similar rules and apply them. If this is happening in your home, you better cut it.

2 - Consequences Of Acts Need To Be Fulfilled

It is almost obvious that if you spoke, they must comply. Therefore, if you have established a rule and said what would be the consequence if the limit was broken, you should put it into practice. It is logical, and in this way, the child will know that you are not speaking for speaking and will respect what you have established without questioning.

However, just as a consequence cannot be "let go," they should not last for long, months, for example, or be permanent. The child needs to be aware of why he was punished. If the punishment is for an indeterminate time, it will come an hour that she will no longer know the reason and will feel wronged.

3 - Rules For Young Children

Many parents are afraid to set rules and limits for small children, but to begin with, this process of education as soon as possible allows children to respect parents at the exact moment of each stage of their life. And believe me, even the young at a very young age already understand what you mean.

Start by imposing rules such as the right time to eat, take a shower, to go to bed. Do everything exactly the same way, every day. Surely you will have fewer problems when you need to send your children to school or do your homework, for example, because they will know you are not kidding.

4 - No Repetitions

You established the rule and applied it. He explained the acts and consequences to his son and made him understand everything right. All right. Now, let the child watch over and take care of one's behavior. Nothing of repeating the same rule at all times, tiring the child and even himself. This will often end up making your child want to see what happens if she breaks that rule so fixed. And if he does, go back to tip 2 of that list: apply the consequence firmly. So, you will be showing to the child that everything he said is valid and that you give the final word.

5 - Limit Age For The Rules

Some parents will ask themselves: should I set limits until my child is at what age? This is relative, and each family has its own culture; each child has his way of acting. But definitely, there is no age limit to stop applying the rules. This should happen as long as the children depend on their parents. From babies to adulthood, if they live under your roof, your kids need you in some way. So rules need to be put in place for a good coexistence, without them overriding your authority. When they are independent and self-reliant, they will set the rules of their own home.

6 - Establishing The Rules

You do not have to create a rule, establish it, but when you apply it, end up seeing that it is a failure. So it is very important to see and revise the limits as often as necessary so that when it comes to putting them into practice, you can show the children exactly what they did and what rules they broke.

Faulty rules are dangerous because children always end up finding a way to circumvent what you have set up, and then you will not have to argue. It is good for parents to make the rules together, even if they are separate. Thus, the child will know that what is worth in one's house is also worth in the house of the other.

7 - Parent Involvement

Depending on the age of your child, he or she may not have discernment of what is right and wrong, and it is up to you to set boundaries. However, from the age of the child to adolescence, they know exactly what they do, what is good or bad, what is according to their demands or not, anyway. Therefore, it may be interesting that they participate in the definition of rules and limits. What happens if they do this or that, what their opinion about some acts, what they think about what you think is wrong, among other things. However, make it clear that it is you who gives the final word and determines the rule in your home.

8 - Be Persistent

Be consistent and consistent in rules. If you break the limits yourself, you end up losing credibility with your children. It seems obvious that they will think, "If he himself could not keep what he said, what can he say about me?" The firm wrist is the watchword for a good education. Create rules consistently so that it fits into the family's everyday life and that everyone living under one roof can collaborate with the child's education. Each family has its reality, and it is very important that the boundaries fit perfectly so that you also do not make your child have a justification for failure.

9 - Visits To Children

If you establish a rule for your child, it will also apply to friends who visit them inside your home. And you should make sure the child or teen explains the rules to other people so that the whole family is not misunderstood, and everyone can live together harmoniously.

Two examples: If you do not want your children to play on the couch, they should tell their friends that it is forbidden in your home. Or if you do not allow your teen to consume alcohol inside your home, you need to make sure their friends know that the party at your house will not have anything of the kind.

10 - In And Out Of Home

Before leaving home, remind your children that the same rules you apply there, are also valid for when they are out. Make it clear that if a boundary break occurs when you are in someone's home, the consequences will apply when they arrive, with no chance of escape. And, if necessary, do so. Try to talk to the child's grandparents, so they do not allow things you do not like, like eating in front of the TV, for example. If something like this happens, remind your children that it happened only once because the grandparents left, but it will not happen again, not here or at your house.

Establishing rules, imposing limits, and applying consequences to children, especially when they are small, can be tricky and even painful for parents. But this will result in responsible adults who know how to respect the world in which they live. A service that parents provide their children with a medium and long-term result.

Conclusion

Understanding the behavior of your toddler may not be the easiest thing to do, however, with a little effort and the right guidance you will be able to raise your kid in a way you will be proud of. Parenting is not something you learn to master overnight, it's an ongoing process, and the more time you invest in getting it right, the more obstacles you'll face! That's not a bad thing. It is an indication you are eager to learn more and improve as a parent.

This book is crafted for you to address some of the most common problems you will face as a parent and help you to deal with it more effectively.

While we have covered a lot of information regarding children and toddlers and their behavior, you need to remember that every child is different and what works like a charm for one kid may prove to be ineffective for your kid. That doesn't mean these techniques aren't helpful. It just means you need to customize the technique a little to benefit your child. As a parent, you know your kid better than anyone else. With the information in this book and your expertise, you should be able to come up with a plan that works well for you and your child!

Do let us know how this book helped you by leaving a review. This will encourage eager parents to make the right purchase.
Happy Parenting!

More Books In
"Positive Parenting Series"

Easy Newborn Care Tips
Proven Parenting Tips For Your Newborn's Development, Sleep Solution And Complete Feeding Guide

Newborn Care Basics
Baby Care Tips For New Moms

If you haven't already, don't forget to download

your FREE quick guide on children's behaviors.

Please, feel free to write to me at:

\>\> lisamarshall@newcommunicationline.com
\<\<

Made in the USA
Columbia, SC
06 December 2019